FAMILY ACTIVISM

26 in 26
Neighborhood Resource Centers
26 Neighborhood Strategies in a 26 month time frame
A Grant Funded by the LSTA
(Library Services & Technology Act)

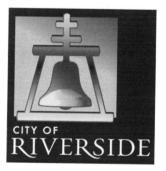

CITY OF
RIVERSIDE

Riverside Public Library

FAMILY ACTIVISM

EMPOWERING YOUR COMMUNITY, BEGINNING WITH FAMILY AND FRIENDS

Roberto Vargas

Berrett–Koehler Publishers, Inc.
San Francisco
a BK Currents book

Berrett-Koehler Publishers, Inc.
235 Montgomery Street, Suite 650
San Francisco, CA 94104-2916
Tel: (415) 288-0260   Fax: (415) 362-2512   www.bkconnection.com

Ordering Information
Quantity sales. Special discounts are available on quantity purchases by corporations, associations, and others. For details, contact the "Special Sales Department" at the Berrett-Koehler address above.
Individual sales. Berrett-Koehler publications are available through most bookstores. They can also be ordered directly from Berrett-Koehler: Tel: (800) 929-2929; Fax: (802) 864-7626; www.bkconnection.com
Orders for college textbook/course adoption use. Please contact Berrett-Koehler: Tel: (800) 929-2929; Fax: (802) 864-7626.
Orders by U.S. trade bookstores and wholesalers. Please contact Ingram Publisher Services, Tel: (800) 509-4887; Fax (800) 838-1149; E-mail: customer.service@ingrampublisher services.com; or visit www.ingrampublisherservices.com/Ordering for details about electronic ordering.

Printed in the United States of America
Berrett-Koehler books are printed on long-lasting acid-free paper. When it is available, we choose paper that has been manufactured by environmentally responsible processes. These may include using trees grown in sustainable forests, incorporating recycled paper, minimizing chlorine in bleaching, or recycling the energy produced at the paper mill.

Library of Congress Cataloging-in-Publication Data
Vargas, Roberto, 1950–
  Family activism : empowering your community, beginning with family and friends / by Roberto Vargas.
    p. cm.
    ISBN 978-1-57675-480-1 (pbk. : alk. paper)
    1. Community development—United States. 2. Community organization—United States. 3. Community activists—United States. 4. Family—United States. I. Title.

  HN90.C6V37 2008
  307.1'4—dc22
                                              2008008093

First Edition
13 12 11 10 09 08   10 9 8 7 6 5 4 3 2 1

INTERIOR DESIGN: Gopa & Ted2, Inc.   COVER DESIGN: Barbara Jellow
COPY EDITOR: Lunaea Weatherstone   PROOFREADER: Henrietta Bensussen
PRODUCTION: Linda Jupiter Productions   INDEXER: Medea Minnich

Dedicated to my grandmother, Mama Cuca,
and my mother, Mama Tita, who taught me
the practice of love in action.

Two outstanding models of family activism
who recently passed on to spirit life:
Antonio "Tony" Salazar (1942–2007)
and Rebecca Victoria Rubi (1949–2007).
Your ability to care for family and community,
and treat all people as *familia*, will continue
to inspire many.

All people doing their part to advance love,
justice, and the Great Turning!

CONTENTS

PREFACE

●●●●●●●●●●●●●●●●●●●●●●●●●●●●●●●●●

Family Activism is about how to create a better world beginning with family and friends. The image of the young girl on the book's cover portrays a glimpse of the vision to which this book is dedicated—connection, hope, joy, and love, a healthy world supporting healthy children. The faint motif on the cover, a symbol from my ancient Mexican indigenous culture depicting "movement that blossoms," represents a central part of the strategy for advancing this vision.[1] Through consciously living to become more loving families, we evolve our culture so as to make it blossom.

This writing was inspired in part by the love for life taught to me by my family. It also arises from my feeling that we all share responsibility to help heal our troubled world and leave it a better place for our children. This book will prepare you with the outlook and tools to increase your family and community power for advancing positive change. It will help you fulfill the vision of "beloved community" that Dr. Martin Luther King, Jr., spoke about—family and friends committed to caring for each other, serving our communities, and healing the world.[2]

The goal is that we become good friends to our families, and family to our friends, purposely encouraging their growth and caring commitment. This way of living requires developing a particular outlook and specific skills, while carefully tending to those around us. Some of us already do this every day, yet all of us can become better at nurturing love and power among the folks we consider family. Those who take up this call to be a family activist are caring people who seek to make all our interactions opportunities to foster spirit, confidence, and social consciousness. They are people who appreciate that love is not only a feeling, it is caring in action.

Family activists seek health and success for their families and all others. They take time to communicate and connect, like the parents who make dinner conversation a family ritual, or the uncle who develops a garden to encourage interaction with his mother and nieces. Family activists create opportunities to foster family connection, like the cousins who organize a "unity circle" to honor their recent high school graduates. They also promote social involvement, like the grandmother who, at every annual Christmas gathering, asks her grandchildren what they have done to serve the community. In thousands of ways like these, family activists create teachable moments to develop the confidence, social awareness, and caring spirit among their loved ones that can help us build joyful families and better communities.

The most powerful medicine we have to heal and evolve our world is our families, when we are inspired to create love and transformation. We can mobilize the power of our networks of family and friends to turn our society away from irresponsible self-destruction. This begins with preparing ourselves to be family activists able to inspire and support our families to be their best. My belief in this approach inspired my writing *Family Activism* to provide you with wisdom about how to connect with your power, your vision, and each other. It is a leadership practice rooted in our hearts and flowering in the world. It is medicine for creating thriving families bettering our world and advancing our human evolution.

There are three parts to this book:

In the world of change agents, one of the guiding concepts is "know why before know how." In other words, understand the philosophy of your strategy before focusing on the "how to." With this in mind, **Part I: The Family Perspective** explains the principles guiding family activism and presents the *Familia* Approach. The chapters in this part remind us why caring for our families is so important, elaborate upon the meaning of family activism, explain the importance of family power to the process of social transformation, and illustrate how we can heal and empower our families.

This part of the book will make you more conscious of what you already know and assist you to deepen your thinking about family power and transformation. Many readers will find that my "Five Principles to Guide Family Activism" reflect much of their own philosophy, as they address fundamental issues about advancing family, community, and social change. Next, the five commitments that define the *Familia* Approach to family activism will, I believe, inspire your increased enthusiasm and capacity for mobilizing family and friends to become a force for change. To illustrate the power of the *Familia* Approach, this part concludes with the story of how my family was able to move from a period of dysfunctional communication to become a loving family that supports each other and advances community service and social change.

In **Part II: Tools for Family Power**, I review principles and tools to enrich your ability to serve your family as a powerful friend, coach, teacher, and facilitator. The first chapter, **Getting Your Act Together**, describes what we must each do to prepare ourselves to live successful lives and be good models of change. The subsequent chapters present and illustrate several essential tools and principles for creating family connection, empowering others, teaching love, and facilitating family gatherings. Given the tremendous potential that family conversations and gatherings have to nurture health and growth, I provide a number of stories that illustrate facilitation tools for making your network of family or friends more connected, inspired, and committed to transformation.

Finally, **Part III: Moving from Family to Community Power** reminds us that family activism is not about engaging in one act of family kindness and then expecting changes to occur. It is about applying your talents consistently over time to assist others to grow, friends to become family, love to blossom, and your community to work together to make a difference. This part contains two chapters illustrating how the *Familia* Approach ultimately can and has influenced positive change in our immediate and larger communities. Stories illustrate how ceremonies, councils, and unity circles are used to evolve more connected communities and a more caring culture. The final chapter provides several illustrations of how beloved communities have been able to affect changes, from inspiring a regional movement that is advancing multicultural respect to creating a project that registered thousands of new voters.

Throughout this book, you will encounter life stories to illustrate the use of various tools, principles, and strategies. Please pay attention to the details of my communication, as I am attempting to demonstrate practices that are typically best learned through direct participation. As my commitment to supporting and inspiring families began with my own family, a number of the stories here involve my parents, brothers, wife, daughters, nephews, and nieces. For this reason, an introduction to my immediate family would be helpful. My parents are Papa Everett and Mama Tita. I am the oldest son, followed by my brothers, Jack, Marcos, and Art. My wife is Rebeca Mendoza, and our daughters are Andrea and Cheli. While our family has expanded, my father and Jack have passed on to spirit life.[3] Many of the stories involve a number of "created families," those networks of friends who have become family to my family. In addition, some stories come from the experience of other family activists. For a number of these illustrations I use footnotes to add acknowledgements or pertinent information. In some cases, names and circumstances have been changed to safeguard people's privacy.

My ultimate intent is to encourage you to apply the tools presented here to facilitate and inspire greater love, community, and service among your family and friends. To assist you in this journey, every chapter ends with several "praxis" questions. Praxis is the idea that creating positive change requires ongoing learning that is best done by reflecting on our experiences and studies to determine how to improve our practice. The questions after each chapter were chosen to provide you with the opportunity to reflect on the reading and your experience, and to bring them together. This practice can be challenging, yet it will support, prepare, and strengthen you in applying the principles and tools with your family and friends. To optimize your learning, I have two suggestions: Begin a journal to note your thoughts and plans that will evolve from the reading, and, most important, identify at least one person to serve as a learning partner, someone with whom you can share and discuss the ideas and questions that will surface. As family activism is invariably about communicating and learning with others, your own process will be more enjoyable and fruitful if you work with a partner.

In my cultural tradition, it is important to introduce oneself to initiate a relationship. Given the relationship I hope to establish with you through sharing the life learnings in this book, I offer the following introduction to tell you about myself, my family, and our evolution of family activism.

ROBERTO VARGAS
Ventura, California
March 2008

INTRODUCTION:
AWAKENING TO ACTIVISM

onsidering the goals and principles I have shared in the preface, you might well ask, are these the unrealistic hopes of an impractical idealist? On the contrary, they comprise the vision and practice of a person dedicated to building a healthy society and a sustainable world. For more than a generation, I have sought to apply love to empower my networks of family and friends so that we can more fully care for and support others. Today, I live with tremendous joy because of the extended family I helped to develop, and because I have found numerous ways to continue expanding my circle of beloved community.

For the past twenty-five years, I have worked as a consultant providing planning, team building, and leadership development to enable proactive organizations to become their best. This work has allowed me to collaborate with fantastic people and organizations throughout the United States, and even places like Canada, Mexico, and Sweden. Whether these organizations are advocacy groups, service agencies, corporations, reservations, or universities, their commonality is dedication to advance good in the world. Most often my job is helping them clarify their vision and become more effective teams in order to more powerfully create positive change.

Culturally, I am a Chicano, a Mexican-American of Indian ancestry, and I am also very much a U.S. citizen.[1] I am proud of the ideals envisioned by our nation's founders, and I am committed to fulfilling our nation's potential to be a global leader of responsible action. As a Chicano whose ancestors were healers, I live committed to community service and social healing. The stereotyping and racism I experienced as a brown youngster instilled within me a passion for justice, respect, and economic fairness for all people. This led me to discover the phenomenal importance of family activism, as I saw that every one of us has family and friends who can be encouraged to become more caring and motivated to help each other and battle for the changes required in our society. We can all be family activists!

Let me tell you a little more about myself and my family by sharing some experiences that have helped shape my path in life. One day, when I was eight years old, I escorted my *Tia* Fina home from her regular visit to our house. There was no sidewalk in our section of town, so I struggled to push my little cousin's baby carriage along the dirt path. Suddenly, a thought came to mind that I proudly shared with my auntie: "When I grow up, I'm going to build a sidewalk from our house to your house." She listened, and I felt her profoundly considering my declaration. She responded, "*Aye, gracias, mijo* (thank you, my son), but a sidewalk would be so expensive, how will you pay for it?" By the tone of her voice, I felt she had no doubt in my conviction, so I continued sharing and developing my vision in response to her occasional, but strategic questions. Our conversation ensued, and before we arrived at her home, I knew that my life's work would be to make the world better.

That day I was glad for the walking time required between our two homes because there was much to think about. My body was keyed up with excitement and discovery. I had connected with my purpose! The questions bubbling up in me were making me think like I never did before and generating many fresh new ideas.

As I thought about this, several teachers came to mind—Jesus Christ, Zorro, and Robin Hood. Jesus was about teaching love. Zorro and Robin Hood were about taking from the rich to give to the poor. I thought, "Maybe when I become an adult I can be like these heroes, but for now, what can I do as a kid?" Reflecting on how hard my parents worked, and being the oldest son of four, I concluded, "For now, the best way I can make the world better is to be a good son and a good person."

For the next several years, this question of how to be a good son and person influenced my behavior and development. Sometimes, when faced with a choice of doing a chore or going to play, I would ask myself, "What is being a good son?" On other occasions, I might reflect on what I had done or not done, and ask, "Was this being a good person?" As a result, I slowly internalized several values that supported me in my core commitment.

At age nineteen, another formative experience arrived as my awareness of injustice in the world intensified. I found a way to visit the Chilean people who were involved in a revolutionary activism to elect a president committed to economic justice. Once there, I made contact with a student organization leading numerous self-help initiatives among the poor and offered my help. Instead of being welcomed, I was told that if I was truly committed to supporting their struggle, I would return to the "belly of the monster" and determine how to create change within my own nation, which was principally responsible for oppressing their country and so many other people around the world. Essentially, they said go home and work to make your own nation responsible. This ultimately led to my returning home and focusing my energies on healing work in my own community, which I will describe more fully in Chapter 1.

Later, another powerful experience added further dimension to my sense of purpose. The young husband of a dear friend unexpectedly and suddenly died. The impact upon Julie and her friends was devastating, and I went to the memorial service to support her. I genuinely looked forward to the officiating priest providing her with the comfort and support she needed. However, the ritual and words spoken felt empty. When the priest stepped down from the pulpit and walked out of the hall, he left all of us more saddened than when we had arrived. A feeling of powerlessness seemed to weigh heavy in the room because we had neither honored our friend who had died nor supported his wife.

I felt a deep anguish for Julie and a strong desire to say or do something to console her and honor her husband, Annu. I didn't know what to do and felt insecure and afraid, but I decided to act. I stood, and words came. I reminded people of how Annu enjoyed being among good friends, and I invited everyone to come forward to make a circle around his coffin. As people joined the circle, I reached out to hold another's hand and others followed. Soon we were all holding hands and our circle started to move of its own accord until we circled Annu several times. I invited people to say final words for him, and heartfelt expressions were shared. Then we broke the circle, and several of us exchanged hugs. However awkward and short, the ceremony was genuine and touched many of us. We felt we had given Annu a little of the love he had always shared with us, and that we had given Julie the support she needed.

For me, this experience brought major revelations. The first was that we have historically transferred to the church and other institutions the authority to administer many of our ceremonies surrounding key life events, yet this doesn't mean that they own these opportunities or that their ministers or priests know how to guide them well. Many of the religious rituals surrounding events such as birthdays, weddings, or death are so steeped in old conventions that they fail to nurture our spirit or inspire us to commit to improving our world. I began to consider that we ordinary people could develop and guide our own ceremonies, and invite guidance from God or our spirit to help us create more inspiring and meaningful rituals. This revelation was liberating and exciting.

Not long after, I had a dream that affirmed my thinking. I found myself alone in the church of my youth with all the pews lined up one behind the other.[2] Then Jesus Christ appeared at the front of the church and told me to remove all the pews and create a space to gather the people. As I worked at moving the pews, he said that my job was to bring people together in circles. While part of me wanted to ignore the dream, the message was unambiguous—bring people together in circles and create ceremonies that foster life and love. This I have sought to do, not as a follower of any church or religion, but as a spiritual person who believes we are all part of the miracle of life.

These are a few of the experiences that prompted me onto the path of family activism, first as a son, then as a father, and now also as a friend and adopted "uncle" to many other families. One of the outcomes of these past thirty years has been to develop the *Familia* Approach to guide caring people to increase love, support, and power within their circle of family and friends. The *Familia*

Approach is a collection of knowledge and tools to encourage love and power within all our relationships, with the goal of bettering our world. The initial motivation for this approach was to support healing required within my own family. Then, as I worked with people throughout my community, our nation, and in other countries, I saw the tremendous need and opportunity we all have within our family networks to teach each other how to be more caring, confident, and skilled in creating positive change in the world.

I also grew to realize the awesome responsibility we all share to address the environmental crisis facing our world. My graduate studies in public health confronted me with the unequivocal evidence that given current population expansion, food and water limitation, and environmental damage, we will not leave our children a healthy, sustainable world. At the same time, I also agree with many leading social philosophers and activists who speak of the Great Turning, the combined efforts of growing numbers of people worldwide who are committed to positive values and a sustainable earth. These efforts are shifting the direction of our society toward becoming a life-sustaining culture.[3]

I have written this book because I yearn to see more joy and well-being for all people, I want to see the health of Mother Earth restored, and I want to know that she will be protected for future generations. This vision will involve millions of people doing their part to transform our culture and society. We can begin with ourselves, and then engage our families, friends, and community. Toward this end, I offer this understanding of family activism and the *Familia* Approach—wisdom and tools to enable you to share in the joy of evolving our human potential for creating a better world.

May the Creator bless us all for our vision and our efforts to honor all creation.

PART I

THE FAMILY PERSPECTIVE

A revolution is not just for the purpose of correcting past injustices. A revolution involves a projection of man/ woman into the future. . . . (It) begins with those who are revolutionary exploring and enriching their notion of a "new man/woman" and projecting the notion of this "new man/ woman" into which each of us can transform ourselves.

— JAMES AND GRACE LEE BOGGS, *REVOLUTION AND EVOLUTION IN THE TWENTIETH CENTURY*[1]

On the level of significance, the family becomes the vehicle through which people can effectively contribute to the well-being of others. . . . Contributing together as a family not only helps those who benefit from the contribution, but it also strengthens the contributing family.

—STEPHEN R. COVEY, *THE 7 HABITS OF HIGHLY EFFECTIVE FAMILIES*[2]

MAKING FAMILY YOUR CAUSE

As activists or people who deeply care about others, we want our society to work for all, and our world to be safe and plentiful for our future generations. For this reason, many of us commit heart and energy to the causes important to us. Maybe our cause is to protect our environment, ensure safe schools and parks for our children, or raise funds to prevent AIDS or cancer. In our passion to make a difference, we often become so focused on our cause that we miss a key principle essential to advancing our vision. The change we desire in the world begins within ourselves and our networks of family and friends.

The idea that we must embody the change we desire is critical, and the "we" includes our circles of family and friends. Whether our commitment is for social justice or a sustainable world, family must be included. For it is among family and friends that we most experience the relationships and support that bring us meaning and joy. Yet, despite the central role that families play in our lives, we often neglect to teach love and change among the people closest to us, to care for and enlist them in creating the better world we seek.

As family activists, our work is about developing ourselves and our ability to facilitate the growth of others. Each of us can foster mutual support and power for positive change among family and friends. Fortunately, once we make this wisdom integral in our interactions with others, we open ourselves to more purposeful living, as people and as activists. We discover that taking care of family and friends is another way of taking care of ourselves and bettering our world. Given your particular family reality, this insight may initially feel challenging, and oftentimes it is. Yet, inspiration will come from knowing you are on the right path and learning valuable tools.

In this chapter, I invite you to view yourself as an activist, and maybe pursue becoming a more mature activist who makes family part of your fundamental perspective. When you choose to view your life with this activist lens, you expand your power to make positive change for your family and communities. Additionally, when you help move your family and friends toward their greater potential, you empower yourself to create greater joy and change than you can imagine. I hope to convey this truth by introducing my understanding of family activism, sharing some personal experiences of discovering its importance, and presenting several ideas that can help you develop your ability to become a more powerful resource and change agent for your family, community, and society.

What Is Family Activism?

Family activism is interacting with those close to you in a way that inspires and prepares them to serve their families and communities as a positive force for change. It is teaching and modeling love among all your relationships, extending acts of caring, thereby encouraging more folks to increase their commitment and time to advancing love and change.

An act of love can transform a relationship in an instant, or it can leave seeds of forgiveness and hope that may manifest within a day, a week, or many years later. It can implant an affirmation that empowers another whom you may never see again to live with courage, or it can kindle a connection with another that can lead to ongoing collaborations to make good happen in the world. This is the type of impact that family activism fosters.

What do the acts of family activism look like? Family activism can include seemingly minor actions, such as initiating a dialogue with your niece to boost her confidence, initiating family meetings to coordinate household chores, or requesting at a birthday party that the group "take a few moments to share with our dear friend why he is truly special to us." Family activism might be having a difficult conversation with a sibling about being a more involved parent, or welcoming a family friend to live in your home until he or she can find a new job. Many of us extend these acts without any thought about our motivation or the implications of our actions. We are just being family or good friends. Yet I believe these acts should be affirmed as a form of activism because they contribute to bettering our world, certainly for the folks immediately involved, and maybe for others we may never know about. And if we do these acts with an ounce of added mindfulness about their activist quality, we can potentially multiply many times over their impact in advancing love and change.

The dialogue with your niece can be the first of a lifelong series of conversations to support her leadership development. The family meeting to take care of business can be designed to also nurture a deeper family connection or to evolve an ongoing practice of analytical thinking about our political environment. Similarly, the sharing at the birthday party can be done so that participants leave feeling touched by love and inspired to increase love in their lives.

How do these acts advance social change? To create a society that truly supports life requires that many of us become less selfish and disconnected, and more caring and powerful. These major changes entail evolving our ability to feel, think, and act in more loving ways. With inspiration and mindfulness, we can learn to live and interact with each other so that we are continually cultivating a feeling of connection and a desire to support each other's well-being. As more of us strengthen our caring instinct and learn to accept our power to create change, we can become a more caring culture able to create changes in all facets of our life, from the way we treat those around us to the political and social priorities in our country.

I will draw on personal experiences to illustrate how activism directed to supporting family and friends can lead to both healthier families and social change. Within my family of birth, I worked with my parents and brothers to develop a culture of mutual connection and support so that we became both a healthier family and one very much involved in community service. The result is that between us we have touched numerous people and created dozens of programs and campaigns that have improved the lives of many.[1] The same is true for the family Rebeca and I have created with our children, in which the methods of family activism have enabled us to better support each other and also be an influence of love and change in our daily personal, community, and work lives.

Finally, much of what I learned from my own family blossomed into even greater outcomes among our extended *familia*. Being a family-oriented person living hundreds of miles away from my family of origin required me to develop and expand my family. Within our new family network of over a dozen and a half families and individuals, I became the recognized facilitator of "family councils" or "unity circles" for special family gatherings such as anniversaries, birthdays, graduations, weddings, and funerals. In essence, my role as a family activist was to create sacred time for family and friends to express their truth, whether it was heartfelt words to honor another or dialogues to learn from each other's experience. Together, we developed traditions for gathering as community in ways that were inspiring, healing, and instructive. Now we get to enjoy interacting with a new generation of young people raised in the tradition of family connection and community service.

These young people are now inspiring us. Many of them are working as teachers, counselors, planners, and community advocates, or do their occupational work and then volunteer in activities that advance community betterment. Many have incorporated into their community service the principles and practices for community building that grew out of our shared experience. These are examples of how family activism that nurtured connection and inspiration among family and friends resulted in the development of more people doing their part to advance social change.

There are more impacts. When we develop a pool of family and friends who share similar vision, commitments, and appreciation for "building community from the family out," together we can become a force to influence even larger circles of community. Various combinations of members of our beloved community have been able to initiate campaigns, organizations, and projects with results like better education, increased multicultural respect, youth leadership development, community empowerment, and peace advocacy. As individuals and families we learned to apply activism within our own family circles to inspire and empower each other to make family and community life better. It's this type of living, doing, and thinking that constitutes family activism.

Multiple Influences for Multiple Effects

When we think of the impacts of family activism, it is important to keep in mind the principle of multiple influences for multiple effects. The change we desire in our society does not occur through a simple cause and effect process. One does not inspire another person to create change in the world in a single conversation. Most often there are multiple events that influence people to become conscious of their power and purpose to make the world better. While they begin to learn how to use their power in positive ways, they are influenced by others who are also extending their influence in the world. Central to the art of activism is to recognize this principle, and to trust that what you do will have its impact over time, as the following account illustrates.

The story begins with my relationship with Joel and Judy García, which formed during the Vietnam War era when Joel and I worked together as conscientious objectors organizing health care for the poor.[2] Early in the development of our families, the Garcías evolved the tradition of frequently bringing family and friends together to celebrate important events. I was often asked to facilitate a unity circle during these events to bring people together to do heartfelt sharing, thereby strengthening our sense of community and connection. At one of our gatherings, Bret Hatcher, a fifteen-year-old friend of the García sons, was deeply impacted by the experience. In his own words, this is the story of the birthday ceremony that began his transformation.

> I took the side path to the backyard where the party was going on. I didn't expect anything extraordinary to happen, just another party with my homeboy's family. I saw a lot of people talking, laughing, and kids just running around. Then I heard the drum beat. Roberto, a friend of the García family, was holding a drum, with his wife at his

side burning sage. Someone said, "It's time for the circle." Roberto started speaking, saying that to honor Mario's birthday we were going to do a sage-burning ceremony to create sacred space, and open a window in time to invite our ancestors and even the unborn children to be with us! He also said people were going to be invited to share their thoughts, feelings, and prayers for Mario and the García family. Talking about the sage and ancestors definitely grabbed my attention.

While the sage burned, Roberto said a prayer to each of the four directions—east, south, west, and north. The smell of the sage was different and nice. The prayers and being in a circle felt sacred and special. All this was new to me, but it was comforting, and I could definitely feel my spirit. I started feeling very lucky to be a part of it.

Roberto invited people in the circle to say congratulatory words to Mario and his family. I just listened. People were speaking compliments, and it was all love. I could feel it! It really touched me. People were totally opening up to everyone else and even crying. It was very emotional, and I could feel the power of what was happening. It got me thinking about how the García family had always been good to me. I was feeling a strong love and friendship inside me and wanted to say something. At first I didn't because this wasn't like me. I never talk in front of groups, but I just had to express myself.

I didn't say a lot, but I did tell Mario "happy birthday" and thanked his parents for always making me feel welcome in their home. That meant a lot to me, especially when so many other people judged me by my appearance. The García family not only welcomed me and trusted me, but saw my potential.

When we finished talking, Roberto did a closing prayer and suggested that we all hug the people next to us. I couldn't believe it, but I just started hugging all sorts of people. I was feeling love around me, inside me, and I just let myself go with it. Without a doubt, the experience opened my eyes and heart. It not only changed my life, but it changed the way I looked at life. For the first time, I felt that maybe I had a future, a purpose, and a place where I belonged.

This family ceremony and others that followed helped Bret connect with his spirit and purpose. He became enthused about his new journey. He approached me about wanting to learn more about the ceremony, and later joined a council committed to supporting men to "live with heart." Seven years later, he had minimized his use of alcohol, and by example inspired a number of his contemporaries to temper their party ways, live closer with spirit, and give more of themselves to their families and community. He had accepted both his Mexican and Irish ancestry, and forgiven his parents for not being available during his early years. Twelve years later, Bret and his wife work, go to school, and are conscientious parents to their daughters. Bret also is an activist, learning and teaching about his culture to support others in becoming and living as good people. When he can, he supports young people in their development and the causes of environmental respect, peace, and healthy families. While he attributes his good path and success to many influences, the García family gatherings and my role in facilitating their ceremonies are paramount to him.

The impact that first ceremony had upon Bret, our dialogues that followed, and the commitments he made to live a good life provide an example of the dynamic of multiple causes for multiple effects. All these experiences influenced the parent and activist he has become, and now he is in turn inspiring and supporting the development of others.

Similarly with our other good friends we developed the tradition of making any of our family gatherings an opportunity to organize family circles to nurture connection and inspiration. And, as with Bret, other young and older people have shared how a single family gathering inspired them to be more caring, and to become family activists for their own circles of family and friends. The transformation that occurred in Bret's life was the result of multiple influences over time. Understanding this dynamic, family activists do their

Any gathering can be an opportunity to create circles that nurture connection and inspiration.

part to foster the expression of love in a variety of forms, trusting that positive outcomes will result. Likewise, when we make our networks of family and friends our cause, we become more powerful facilitators of health and transformation for them, our communities, and our world.

Discovering the Obvious Takes Time

Sometimes the most obvious insight eludes us until our minds and hearts are ready to understand. Each of us has a story of how we learned the importance of balancing attention to ourselves, our family, and our community in our journey to create a better world. My personal story revolves around the evolution of my activism, and pivotal in it was my discovery of the importance of making family essential to my cause.

As an eight-year-old youngster I was elated when I first saw my purpose—to create a better world! To me it seemed only fair that other children on my street should enjoy a life as good as mine. If we had food to eat, clean clothes to wear, and no worry about violence, they should also. And I felt that by being a good son and supporting my parents, I was in some way doing my part to make the world better.

When I became a teenager my world expanded, and so did the nature of my activism. Through my church I organized youth to participate in community service, from collecting food or clothing for those in need to providing tutoring to youngsters. Later, when I learned about the causes of injustice, my outrage fueled a new form of activism. I organized students to support the United Farm Workers union in their struggle for economic justice, and to educate our communities to stop our nation's immoral war in Vietnam.

Later still, I had the eye-opening experience in Chile recounted in the preface. After a short time there observing the dedication and power of young people (ages nineteen to twenty-two years) collaborating with the working poor to provide essential housing, electricity, sanitation, education, and medical care, I was inspired. I returned home believing in my power. I also carried a focused question that guided my everyday activities: How can I create positive change in the United States while also earning a living? I finally envisioned a form of employment that would also be my activist work—organizing a counseling center to provide people with skills to take care of themselves and their communities.

I came to Oakland, California, in 1972 with this objective. Joining a local community health agency that shared a similar vision, I soon cofounded and became director of *El Centro de Salud Mental (The Center for Mental Health)*, which was dedicated to social transformation through healing and empowerment.[3] Central to the organizing effort was drawing together a staff committed to reinventing the practice of counseling. Our desire was to provide services to heal our families and inspire them to participate in improving our communities.

At twenty-two years old, I found myself living with the monumental challenges of directing and growing a center while reinventing the practice of mental health service. For inspiration and support, I discovered the power of the Oakland hills. I would climb to different vantage points to meditate on the beautiful panorama of the bay and on my purpose. From here I viewed the community I shared with several million people, the suburban cities to the south, the well-to-do communities across the bay, and the multiple inner city neighborhoods comprising the flatlands. Absorbing this view, my constant question was, how do we advance social change in such a complex and diverse society? As dusk became evening and the sparkle of a few lights became thousands, I would consider that each light represented a different person or family. This often focused my question further. How do we reach all these people and make them activists for social change?

This ritual that I started as a young person continued for more than thirty-five years. Every few weeks, I would climb into the hills to seek inspiration or deeper answers to the perennial question, how do we advance the healing and change required by our communities, our society, and our world? Over the years, my life circumstances and the answers I heard moved my activism into different arenas.

During one period my professional work as a planning consultant enabled me to teach and facilitate positive change for organizations and communities in major cities throughout the United States, and even internationally, as when I worked with the Swedish government to prevent the growth of racism in Sweden. During these times I often observed that the most significant change seemed to happen when numbers of key people congregated to plan, share training, and take actions.

Then life circumstances directed me to another form of active caring. After months traveling the country helping communities to develop innovative counseling programs, I found myself emotionally and physically exhausted. I needed to return to my family home for rest and renewal. When I arrived, I was shocked to discover that my family of parents and brothers was struggling with discord. At first I felt disbelief, because my family had always been a primary source of inspiration. Then a sense of inner contradiction arose. If I truly cared about community, why wasn't I taking care of my own family? I decided to direct my attention and skills to healing the family of my origins.

This shift commenced an ongoing push and pull between focusing attention on my family or on what I considered my more "important" community activism. My prevailing perspective was that supporting family well-being was a distraction from my professional and activist work. Later, I was to learn the importance of integrating both the family and community work, yet this took time and several major life-changing experiences, most importantly the birth of my daughters.

The focus of my consultation practice was providing leadership training, but when my first child was born I realized that real leadership development began with raising babies to believe in themselves and their ability to love. With vital support from my wife, I downsized my consultation practice, set up my office at home, and became an active houseparent. My activism on the home front was focused on developing the confidence of my children and their friends, as I also sought to foster their caring spirit, their interest in learning, and their inquiry skills.

Together with my wife and members of my family, we learned to live a balance that involved taking care of each other and our multiple communities, while contributing to the big-picture social change. Part of this learning process involved many more hikes into the Oakland hills, more frequently with my children, first as youngsters and then as adults. My questions were largely the same, yet often reflecting the inquiries I was hearing from the different communities with whom I worked. How do we fulfill the American vision of being a nation that models our best human values? How do we advance the Great Turning, the current movement to save our world from the path of self-destruction?[4]

During one of these hilltop moments came my big "aha"—*familia-first activism!* The idea surfaced that creating a better world had to start with family. Then another internal voice, the disparaging one, said, "No big deal, everybody knows that." My insecure voice talked me into letting the idea go, but during another reflective occasion, it arose again, *familia first*, and the idea of *family activism* took hold. We must make families our cause. To create a movement that involves people of all classes and communities, every caring person must learn to see themselves as an activist. To create the community and society of our vision, we activists must accept responsibility to encourage our own family and friends to actively care for each other and our world. Ever since then I have sought to deepen my understanding of the power of family activism to advance the healing and transformation needed by our world.

Family Is Most Important to Us

For most people, the combined relationships we call family are as important to us as life. When times are good, whom do we want to share it with? When times are difficult, whom do we seek for assistance? Most often the answer is our parents, siblings, children, and closest friends. They know and care about us; they are most important to us.

Yet, for some reason, within our U.S. American society we often forget this truth. In part, this is the result of the messages we hear: *Success is about taking care of number one. The most important person is you. Life is about getting what you need and want.* But while a focus on our personal needs and success is essential, it is also imperative to recognize the significance of our family. It is time that we own certain truths about family: *I succeed because of the support that I receive. Success is about taking care of each other. When the family is doing well, life is great.*

Family is important to us for many reasons. Family brings us purpose and joy. When we take care of our family, we feel the joy of reciprocating the support we were given. We also feel part of something greater than ourselves that we want to nurture and grow. Supporting the growth and well-being of our family means to be part of our human purpose, to live life and develop our ability to be more human. Toward this end we need our family to survive, enjoy life, and succeed. We need their emotional and financial support to take care of us during our early years and then to position us for success. We need their presence to learn how to be caring people. We need their love to help us grow to love ourselves. We need our family and friends to make life worth living.

Our greatest joys involve sharing with family. It feels good to accomplish our goals, yet it feels even more fulfilling when we can share the triumphs with our family. You can feel happiness in receiving a meal prepared by your mother, or witnessing the excitement of one of the youngsters learning a new skill. These family experiences bring us inspiration and food for our souls, while energizing us to do more for others or pursue being a better person.

We also need support from our families to prepare for the long-term work involved in healing our society. My three brothers and myself have maintained activist lifestyles for at least the last twenty-five years. Ask us how we have been able to sustain our involvement and we will tell you that this largely can be attributed to our *familia*, our family of origin, and later our wives and children. When we were young, the financial support provided by our parents allowed us time for study, church, or community involvement. Later, because of the traditions of communication and family councils we had evolved, we not only had each other for emotional, intellectual, and practical support, we were part of an expanded family of mutual support involving our wives, partners, children, good friends, and our beloved community.

All families, yours and those of your coworkers and friends, can be developed to become a greater source of support and activism. When we invest in making our families our cause, we strengthen our ability to create the change we desire in the world. We increase our numbers, and we have greater inspiration and joy to sustain our efforts.

Activists Are People Who Care

We may think of activists as mostly people who actively organize in their community or who are involved in political advocacy. But I want to expand this understanding and say that all people who actively care for and serve others are activists. Then as caring people or activists our ultimate goal should be to express our love for the people around us as we also pursue the creation of a healthier society. This is what I would call mature activism.

My early activist years were during the late 1960s when an entire generation was marching for civil rights and protesting to end the war in Vietnam. I wore jeans and long hair like most other activists. Unfortunately, most of us got stuck in viewing activism as solely involving radical action directed toward a political or social end. Inadvertently, we squeezed out from our ranks the millions of people who are involved in other forms of active caring.

An activist is a person who cares and takes positive action. It is the person who realizes that a dozen kids may not get a chance to play soccer this season unless they find a coach, so she volunteers. It is the person who stops by his neighbor's house once a week to ensure a warm dinner for an elder. It is the young person who, hearing racist remarks by her peers, announces that until her friends are more respectful of others she chooses to have lunch elsewhere.

The caring actions of these people are invaluable because they make our communities a better place—those who are hungry are fed, those who are sick are comforted, young people are provided opportunities to develop, and elders are made to feel valued. By serving others they are shaping and modeling the values we desire within our community, such as love, respect, and justice. These activists, whether they call themselves Christians, good neighbors, or simply caring folks, are living these values, and in the process teaching and inspiring others to live them also.

I don't know how my mother found time, yet I remember us frequently visiting elders or people who were ill when I was young. The routine became familiar. As we arrived, first there was the reminder from my mom, "We are here to bring food, so, please, you are not hungry." Next, after a quick survey of the situation, she had me cleaning the yard, watering the plants, or running off to purchase food or medicine. Finally, before leaving we were invited to share in a prayer circle.

My mother cared about and served others because she was a loving person. There was no political or social objective to her service, just the expression of her loving concern. Because of her, my brothers and I developed similar values. Then, given opportunities to study that our parents did not have, we developed deeper understanding of the causes of many of our community's problems. We learned how companies frequently exploit their workers, how corporations promote consumerism and waste, and how special interests manipulate our political system for profit while ignoring pressing needs for health care, affordable housing, and environmental protection. Our responsibility became to advance the change required to address these big problems and their underlying causes. Our challenge was to live as mature activists—to engage in both present-moment caring and the work of advancing a better society.

Maturing the character of your activism involves expanding your idea of service in distinct directions. Those of us involved in extending random acts of kindness, like my mother, could potentially enrich our service by also seeking to understand more deeply the forces that undermine the well-being of our communities, and then possibly using our credibility to engage those we serve in conversations about our responsibilities to minimize energy waste, confront racism, or end war. Similarly, many big-picture activists could advance a better society by learning to look after those who need attention, to be more respectful and kind in all our relationships.

Making family our cause provides both service-oriented and change-oriented activists a means to grow and better complement each other's efforts. Service activists may find caring for family easy since it involves extending kindness, which they often enjoy doing. Their challenge is thinking and acting for the long-term survival of our larger community. Change activists, who may find it easier to focus on the big problems, need to engage with family and friends to "keep it real," and strengthen their capacity to relate to the daily concerns of people. Because we care, we must make family our cause, with the vision of together becoming a stronger force for positive change.

PRAXIS

1. Why is your family important to you? How has your family influenced who you are becoming? How have you influenced your family?
2. When did you first discover the love and concern you have for others? What are you currently doing to advance the well-being of your family and friends?
3. Viewing yourself as a family activist, what might be your next steps to develop your abilities and mature your activism?

2

PRINCIPLES TO GUIDE
FAMILY ACTIVISM

● ●

My earnest involvement in family activism, even though I
didn't identify it as such, began when I was twenty-six years
old. That is when I decided to consciously apply my knowledge
about communication and organizing to make my family more
united, nurturing, and mutually supportive, including my networks
of friends and colleagues whom I also considered as family. My
thought was to strengthen my immediate community so we could
be more available to create positive change in our society. During
these years, there was no articulated idea of family activism, just a
handful of friends believing that a better world somehow begins
with healthier families, so we just learned from our doing. Now, as
I reflect on my activism thirty years later, I recognize that I was
largely guided by five key foundational principles.

These five principles represent my basic philosophy about how to
advance a world that works for all, beginning with co-powering
family and friends to become part of the force of love and transformation. By no means are these principles fully inclusive of all ideas
required for change and transformation, yet they provide an important beginning for those who seek to make our families, communities, and societies better for everyone. They provide an understanding of the "know why" that underlies the methods and tools
imparted in this book.

PRINCIPLES THAT GUIDE

FAMILY ACTIVISM

1. **View everyone as family.** Recognize that everyone you care for and who cares for you is family.
2. **Care for family.** Support everyone in getting what they need for health, growth, and happiness.
3. **You and your family be the change.** You and your family model the change you desire in the world.
4. **Teach positive family power.** Teach love and caring to create positive family power.
5. **Encourage vision and transformation.** Advance social transformation through vision and personal change.

View Everyone as Family

Recognize that everyone you care for and who cares for you is family.

My view of family activism is based upon several ideas of *familia* popular within my culture. These include the belief that everyone we care for and who cares for us is family, and that being family means "being for all our loved ones." When we deepen our understanding of these seemingly simple concepts, we can more fully grasp the spirit and vision of family activism.

Dr. Phil McGraw, a psychologist who works with family issues on television, writes in his book *Family First*, "Among all words in the English language, none means more to human beings than 'family'."[1] Family is often our prime reason for living and working. Family brings us joy and happiness and inspires us to grow. Words are important because they shape our thinking, and I believe we can learn tremendous lessons about being family from other meanings inherent in the word and experience of *familia*. For example, in my culture the word *familia* revolves around the central idea of "caring for everyone you love." Your friends are your family, and your fam-

Everyone you care for and who cares for you is family. We organized events to make our neighborhood feel like family and community.

ily includes your community. Just as you desire well-being and success for yourself, you desire the same for family and friends. This idea calls upon us to actively care for the well-being of each person we love through our thoughts, words, and deeds, and with responsibility, love, and respect.

When my wife and I recently decided to move in with my mother to support her quality of life, given her stroke and increasing age, I shared the news of our move with friends and neighbors. A comment from Mrs. Duffy, our new eighty-year-old neighbor, was thought-provoking. She said, "That's what I admire about you people [meaning Latinos]. Family is special and you folks do for your family in ways that a lot of us don't, but should." The question came to mind, "Is the quality of being family different in my culture than in others?"

I thought about her statement for some time, and finally decided that I agree. It's true that among the diverse cultures and societies in our world, many maintain unique best practices from which other cultures can learn valuable lessons. Perhaps my combined indigenous and Latino culture has particular gifts to impart about how to be more caring families. What if our U.S. American society decided to encourage the best practices surrounding the idea of *familia*? This could certainly bring us greater family and community cohesion, appreciation, and responsibility.

In English, "family" typically connotes one's immediate and extended blood relationships and spouses. In contrast, *familia* in popular usage tends to have two equally significant meanings, one conveying who is family, and the other expressing significant values of being family. For us, *familia* includes an expanding circle of relations, beginning with those we consider to be immediate family because we are present for each other. This usually includes our core family and dear friends with whom we share commitment and support. From here our circle of *familia* can expand to include all our primary relatives, our larger extended family, close friends of our family, and even ancestors and our children over the next seven generations. This is why every time we say we are going to have a *familia* gathering, we need to clarify how much of the family we are inviting.

Familia also represents an attitude and value system that is about deeply caring for those you consider family. Within my indigenous and Latino cultures, *familia* is very much an attitude about connection, commitment, respect, love, and purpose. This is illustrated through the multiple connotations that are conveyed in the statement, "*somos familia,*" which gives further insight into the spirit of family activism. The literal translation for *somos familia* is "we are family," yet when the statement is made to another, regardless of whether that person is related, the implied message is, "We are connected, and we are here to support each other's survival and success." In a slightly different context, when one is responding to another who has just extended thanks, the sentiment behind "*somos familia*" can be interpreted as, "We have enough love to share."

Familia also connotes such values as respect and active caring. When a son or daughter leaves to visit another family member, one parent may offer the reminder, "*Somos familia,*" which serves as a powerful signal of values important to their family. In my family it meant, "Don't forget to be caring and respectful." In other words, when you arrive at your grandmother or uncle's home, remember to extend greetings on behalf of the family and check to see if they might need any groceries or help around the house. Being *familia* is being available, and even proactive, in extending support to each other. Don't wait to be asked. Observe, note needs, and extend support. This is active caring.

This active caring was prevalent in my extended family and community experience, in part because as Mexican-Americans we were, and often still are, a people struggling to survive within a society that often views and exploits us as cheap labor. Thus, many of us grew up in families where a dominant value was supporting each other to succeed, while also pursuing justice, healthy community, and social change. This is often referred to as being *familia*, yet for everyone who desires to create positive change beginning with family, it can be referred to simply as family activism. Family activism is living as *familia*, which is sharing support with our expanded circle of relationships as we encourage everyone to do their part to advance family and community well-being.

Given your particular cultural and social reality, your practice of family activism will have its unique qualities. Naturally, there are differences in the communication and meeting styles amongst people from different backgrounds and locations. The challenge for you will be to identify and value your unique style of family activism. While my activist practice is greatly influenced by my Chicano experience, my commitment is to share with you tools that will serve people of any culture who desire to nurture love within their family circles while also increasing their power to pursue positive change in their community and society. What I call the *Familia* Approach includes principles and tools for family activism that can be used by all people who wish to nurture the caring instinct within their children, make their family events occasions of community connection, joy, inspiration, and commitment, or who desire to cultivate within their friendship and professional networks values and practices reflective of being *familia*.

With the above in mind, I request that when you see the word "family" in this book you consider it to include your more expanded circle of caring relationships and the best values and practices we can associate with being family. So "family" here will mean all your friends and loved ones, the feeling of connection and love you have for them, and being mutually supportive and community responsible. Here, family or *familia* is about being the "beloved community" that Dr. Martin Luther King Jr. spoke about. It is being family with each other as we struggle to increase justice and love in the world.

Care for Family

Support everyone in getting what they need for health, growth, and happiness.

In large part, family activism begins with taking care of your own family. Do what you have to do to ensure they have the basics for healthy living today and, to the degree possible, for tomorrow.

Twelve million families in the United States worry about their next meal.[2] Given the wealth in this nation, this is inexcusable. We need to do more to take care of our families. Yes, parents could do more to care for children, yet, given the income and time required to raise healthy children, all of us, from relatives to friends to neighbors, need to do more than our share. Parents cannot do it alone; they and their children need our support.

As parents, we have the primary responsibility to ensure that our children receive everything they need to grow, develop, and succeed. At the most basic level, this means generating enough income to provide our children with food, clothes, and a safe home. For growing numbers of families, that requires that both parents (where there are two) work and often at more than one job. Yet our children also need love, attention, guidance, and support. From us adults, they need to know and feel that we care for them. They need us to be involved, asking essential questions about their welfare. Are they eating healthy food? Are they exercising? Are they getting good support for their learning and education? Do they have emotionally supportive relationships? Do they have a plan for their success? And then, of course, they need us to actually provide this support.

For many of us, particularly the underpaid working parents or single-parent heads of households, our family activism consists of paying the bills, coordinating everyday life, and extending the love

Parents and their children need our support.

and attention that we can. Our activism manifests by taking care of our family, for which we should feel pride. However, we should also invite our uncles, aunts, grandparents, friends, and neighbors to make their contribution. Family is "all our relations," and when families include children or elders, it becomes part of our responsibility to extend support to them. As uncles, aunts, and friends we can do this by making quality time for the young ones, getting to know them, and nurturing their development, or occasionally providing practical assistance that may be needed.

In caring for our families, it's also important to consider the wider community and the world the young will inherit. For those of us who have more resources, it is only fair that we contribute some effort to both ensure that our family relations are receiving necessary support, and that we learn and do our part to make our communities safer, our society more just, and our world more sustainable.

You and Your Family Be the Change

You and your family model the change you desire in the world.

This principle echoes the teachings of Mahatma Gandhi: "You must be the change you want to see in the world."[3] If your desire is for justice and respect in the world, then actively seek to cultivate justice and respect in all your relations. If your desire is for all people to live with health and joy, then seek to advance health and joy in all your activities. To this teaching, I would add that as you pursue the changes you desire, also consider how to care for yourself and family. This has several implications. The social change we seek is complex and full of challenges and struggles that require us to sustain a long-term commitment. Consequently, it is important to care for yourself with attention to balance, spirit, health, and humor to ensure you last the distance required.

You must balance taking care of yourself, your family, and your community commitments. This is best done by developing relationships of support within your family for the activist or service work that you do. Take time to help your parents or siblings understand the nature of your work and why you are committed to it, and ask for their help. All forms of activist work are easier when family and friends understand and respect your efforts and have the opportunity to periodically lend support, whether it is time, money, prayers, or an occasional word of appreciation.

Everyone in your family counts. To develop a society committed to ending hunger, homelessness, and joblessness requires the caring spirit, creativity, wisdom, and concerted effort of many people. We cannot afford to lose a single dedicated person, nor can we ignore the value of aiding family and friends to be more socially responsible. While some may resist participating in change, we can maintain our persistence in supporting their growth and commitment to service. If their time for growth is not at hand, the family activist pours caring attention upon others, and continues to model and work for the change we desire in the world.

Teach Positive Family Power

Teach love and caring to create positive family power.

Positive family power is love, and developing this power within our families is essential to family activism. Look for opportunities and ways to encourage love for self and others. This love includes taking caring action on behalf of others—cooking a meal for a tired parent, collecting contributions for workers on strike, or supporting the effort to end toxic dumping in the communities of the working poor. What makes it love is that we do it because we care for others, and we know our actions will add another ounce of fairness, joy, and respect in the world. As we extend our love, we also do it with mindfulness that our actions model caring that can inspire and increase family power to achieve positive change. In this section, I would like to deepen our understanding of *porvida* love and family power.

About Porvida *Love*

Like many activists, I resisted recognizing the primary role that love has in social change work. Since I was young, I was motivated by the teachings of Jesus Christ, and as a young adult, by the quote on the poster of Che Guevara that hung on my bedroom wall: "At the risk of sounding ridiculous, let me say that a revolutionary is motivated by deep feelings of love." Yet, when one of the most renowned activist teachers in my community, Pablo Sanchez, suggested that I could be much more effective if I acknowledged that my work was about teaching love, I walked away disappointed and frustrated at his naivety.[4] My thought was that our work has to be about people empowerment, and what does love have to do with that?

At that time, I was nearly thirty years old, and for half of my life I had been doing individual and community empowerment work throughout California. The word "love" had always felt too sentimental and tangential to me. I saw the appeal to love more as a ploy to direct people away from necessary social change activism. Fortunately, life provided me a number of experiences that led me to understand the profound nature of what I call *porvida* love—love for life and justice—and its importance in my activism.

Before discussing *porvida*, it's important to understand love itself. For this purpose, it's helpful to utilize several words from other cultures, given the dearth of English words available to fully describe the multiple facets of love. When most of us think of love, several types typically surface, such as parental love for a child, romantic love that occurs between two people, or the love that derives from friendship, which the ancient Greeks called *philia*. There are other profound concepts of love that our U.S. culture seems to overlook, such as *agape*, a Greek term meaning a love for God and humanity, or what indigenous Hawaiians call *aloha*, a love of life that emanates from our spirit and seeks to manifest itself in the joy of our every breath.[5]

About the nature of *agape* love, Dr. Martin Luther King, Jr., wrote, "*Agape* is understanding, creative, redemptive good will for all men. Biblical theologians would say it is the love of God working in the minds of men. It is an overflowing love which seeks nothing in return. And when you come to love on this level you begin to love men not because they are likable, not because they do things that attract us, but because God loves them. . . ."[6]

Agape represents our unconditional love for humanity. It says, love your neighbor as yourself and be willing to sacrifice your life for them. It is not sentimental, but a profoundly courageous and giving love. It is a love lived by caring people who desire to make the world better for all, the love that Dr. King labored to make the center of the civil rights movement. In the 1958 battle between the people of Montgomery, Alabama, and the offensive policies of segregation, the protesters stood for justice and restrained themselves from responding with violence even as police and civilians beat them or unleashed dogs on them and their brothers, sisters, and children. They drew courage from their love for community and their commitment to justice, to use the power of nonviolent action to win their battles, thereby inspiring a national movement for civil rights.[7]

We should never forget the power of love that was demonstrated by this beloved community, supporting each other to survive as they remained dedicated to their vision for justice. Their efforts keep us mindful that our capacity for love and action is often much greater than we realize. Drawing from their example, we too can step into our courage and bring this force of love into our everyday actions. This may involve taking the risk to speak against racism or oppression of women, extending assistance to a neighbor, or simply doing the right thing despite peer pressure.

Porvida provides yet another face of love. In my circle of healers, mostly from the Latino community, we evolved the concept of *porvida* love to describe the profound commitment that resides within people of all cultures who seek to be fully for life, justice, and the well-being of Mother Earth. We derived *porvida* from the Spanish words *por vida*, literally meaning "for life," which in popular usage conveys the meaning of making a commitment for the entirety of our lives. Thus, *porvida* love is about loving life and humanity so profoundly that we seek to make our everyday actions advance love and respect in the world.[8]

Porvida love is a commitment to life, love, justice, and the evolution of our spirit and humanness. It is love that arises from the core of our spiritual being. It is our passion for life that deeply and fervently embraces the totality of life, including all people, life forms, our environment, and all our relations. It is our inner calling to be compassionate, caring, and in active relationship with all of life. *Porvida* love is idealistic, optimistic, and responsible. It is love that recognizes that we are humans in evolution, continually growing our capacity to love and to create relationships and systems that support our ability to be better people. *Porvida* love is about courageously seeking to evolve all that is positive.

When we feel love, our desire is to allow that energy to expand. When love resides within a family, members immediately respond to the needs of others and act to support each other in achieving success. When there is abundant love, the family has increased energy to care for others and their community.

Whether we call it *agape*, *porvida*, or spirit essence, our inherent nature is to be for life and love. Our challenge is to connect more with our loving essence, further our ability to live in a positive way, and support others in accepting and evolving their inherent goodness. Family activism is fundamentally about learning and teaching such love.

About Family Power

One of the principal goals of family activism is to develop our power, our personal and collective ability to take positive action. Many people have difficulty even talking about power, assuming that power is always negative, that it's about control and about one person being superior to another, or that power corrupts. In fact, the core definition of power is the "ability to act," stemming from the Latin word *posse*, meaning "to be able." Power is the ability to take action to produce desired results or to accomplish what is important to us. This can be anything from fulfilling a resolution to develop yourself, supporting the success of your sibling, or organizing a local campaign to ensure healthy water.

Our families need greater power. Consider what is vital to you— the ability for loved ones to achieve personal success, family well-being, safe environments, responsive government, and knowing that your children will inherit a healthy and sustainable world. We need to develop among family and friends the personal and collective power to transform aspirations such as these into goals, and then to make them happen. This is family power, our individual and collective ability to apply ourselves to be a positive force for taking care of each other and our communities.

Developing family power begins by nurturing the self-confidence of all people within our network to accept their capacity to act and effect change on behalf of themselves and their families. In our society, there is such a dearth of positive validation that most young people and adults only manifest a fraction of their power because they don't believe in their self-worth. Consequently, one core responsibility of family activists is to continually find ways to build the self-esteem and personal power of family and friends. We can do this in every conversation. At a family gathering, we can take note of the young, from toddlers to teenagers, and seek opportunities to interact with them and build their self-esteem. Whether it is with young people or adults, we can converse in a way that affirms, evolves, and develops their power.

Family members who believe in their personal power can then mobilize their family to care for each other in significant ways. The Gonzales family of Chicago provides an example. While recognized within their community for the various organizations and projects they initiated, they have also developed within their family culture the power for mutual support, as evidenced by a recent crisis. Upon hearing the devastating news that their cousin's wife was diagnosed with cancer, the extended family was mobilized, and within hours, prayer circles were organized and a number of cousins had committed to support the family, which had three young children. Donna, one of the organizers, admits to having spoken to her cousin, Mark, perhaps only once over the last several years, yet she said, "When family needs you, you just step up. Sure, we all have full schedules, but what's more important than those children getting all the love and support they need?" This is family power directed to family well-being.[9]

Family power also exists in the commitment of a family to support each other to engage in community action. Over the years, my brother Marcos directed several community-based organizations, and then developed a new organization that has brought community, faith, and labor networks together to pass four municipal living wage ordinances and other local policies. This work has resulted in increased income for more than 5,000 families and the formation of numerous multicultural relationships that are demonstrating to our community that diverse people can join together to support progressive causes and candidates. Marcos credits his wife, family, and friends for enabling his accomplishments, along with his many activist collaborators. Since his early adulthood, his mother, brothers, and then wife and children have provided a spectrum of practical, financial, and emotional support to allow him to focus on his studies and his community activism. Our prevailing attitude is, "Supporting Marcos is supporting the community, so let's extend the help that we can." This is the family power of mutual support that aids community action.[10]

Finally, there is the form of family power where family and friends directly work together to support the community. We probably all have examples of this form of power. Someone in our network decides to initiate a local project to serve our community or to run for a political office. Then we, as family or close friends, either volunteer or are drafted to get involved. Before we know it, we are taking care of each other's children or using our various family gatherings to support action and planning on behalf of our project or campaign. This is family power directed to community action. As family activists, we teach and model love so as to develop family power.

Encourage Vision and Transformation

Advance social transformation through vision and personal change.

We each must ask ourselves about the vision we have for our ideal family, community, and world. I believe most of us desire a healthy and caring family and a society that works for everyone. But what would this actually look like? Key to actualizing such a desire is to first clarify and hold the vision, put it forth in ideas and pictures, and then work for change, keeping it in mind and making it our goal in all that we do. This process begins with oneself, then expands to include our family relationships, our culture, and the numerous institutions that comprise our social reality.

About Vision

Before we explore vision, let's take a brief stock of our social reality. Some of us live in communities where street violence is an everyday concern, the air is contaminated, healthy food is unavailable or too expensive, and families are overworked and underpaid or struggling with unemployment. Many of us also share concerns about global warming, the poisoning of our air, soil, and water, corporate greed that is driving salaries down, and the ongoing war that is sending young men and women to death while draining our tax dollars that could be used to ensure a better life for all our families.

Because all these issues and more require resolution, many of us are already working to advance safer communities, environmental protection, and peace. This is absolutely great. Now, to optimize our efforts for change, we need to approach our activism in these and other areas with our larger vision in mind. Whether our concern is protecting our environment, improving our schools, or halting violence, when we participate with our vision guiding us we are more effective in moving forward all the other related changes required to create a better world, including how we communicate and work with each other.

Every day I want as many of my activities as possible to advance my vision of a better society. For this reason, many years ago I made a list of all the ways I wanted our nation and world to improve. It included everything from clean air, water, and soil, and responsible population growth, to families knowing how to live in respect. Then I selected a couple of short phrases that captured the totality of the list that I could turn to whenever I needed focus and inspiration.

Sharif Abdullah, an internationally recognized trainer on cultural transformation, writes about creating "a world that works for all."[11] I love this idea. It articulates my vision simply and helps me gauge my everyday actions to ensure that I am living and working in alignment with my hopes. I also use the concepts of "a healthy society," "a better world," or "heaven on Earth." My favorite is "heaven on Earth" because I believe bringing this about is within our power. I was raised in the Christian tradition, and for me the teachings of Jesus Christ advise us to make heaven happen in our lives each day. We have been blessed with all the intelligence and resources we need to make this happen for ourselves, our families, and the larger human community. I try to approach every interaction and decision with this attitude so that the outcome, however great or small, serves to achieve the vision of heaven on Earth.[12]

Having a key phrase that captures your larger vision can provide you with inspiration to persevere and to inspire others. Develop a list of all those qualities you desire to see in our world, and then select an overall vision phrase that resonates for you. Once you identify your phrase, look around and see where the vision is already living. You might see it in the way an adult extends support to a child, in a bus system that effectively transports people where they need to go, or in the beauty of a healthy tree. While observing these images, bring to mind your vision phase, articulate your personal commitment, and feel confident that people of good will are helping to make it happen.

The work of creating change is challenging. For that reason we all need and deserve the inspiration that comes from knowing that our aspirations for society are more than just "fixing problems." Ultimately, your role as a family activist will be to clarify your vision, to inspire, and to allow yourself to be inspired.

About Transformation

In this context, transformation means all change and development intended to make us more loving and caring, our society more respectful, and our world more life sustaining. Much of this book is about tools for facilitating and supporting positive change and transformation, but here I want to underscore the idea that the transformation we desire for our society begins within our families, and introduce the ways in which this can happen.

The transformation begins with our personal development and then requires our support for family change. A first step might involve honest inquiry about yourself. This means asking such questions as, "How can I be a more effective model of love and a supporter of transformative change? How can I move from being self-centered to being more caring for others, or from an attitude of pessimism to increased optimism?" Each of us has our own changes to be made, which might include being more giving rather than selfish, courageous rather than timid, or a better listener rather than a constant talker. Asking these questions and committing to examine and change our attitude or behavior is the first transformation work that needs doing. And as we work on our own transformation, we learn lessons to support similar change among our family and friends.

To advance the positive change we desire for our families, our role is to support our family members and friends in their development, and our family network as a whole in its ability to be mutually supportive. For many of us this may require both assisting our families to resolve existing dysfunctions, and the conscientious effort to encourage and support the personal growth of those close to us. First, let's consider what transformation can look like and how it can be supported.

My grandfather demanded that his five-year-old son work like an adult and physically abused him when he couldn't. That child became my father, who cared for his children and never physically punished us. This was a transformation. While my father demonstrated his love for his children by financially supporting us, he didn't know how to touch or listen to us very well. Yet we learned from him, and much from our mother, particularly about love. Consequently, my brothers and I became more affectionate fathers and uncles to our children, thereby advancing the transformation.

Generation to generation transformation in which we learn to become better people is an important contributor to change, yet as family activists our desire is to speed up the process. A recent example is when my sister-in-law spoke with me regarding the childhood stories I was sharing with the children, concerned that a couple of these stories tended to diminish the image of one of my brothers. After reflecting on her comments, I acknowledged that my perspective was not the most positive, and I revised the stories to be more respectful of all my brothers. This may seem an insignificant change, yet it has led to other changes that support my evolution and my ability to be more transformative within our family.

Every improvement in attitude and practice is part of the transformation. Our responsibility is to believe that change is always doable, and to recognize that each requires its own period of time. Some transformations require years, while others occur in just moments. Our task is to learn more about transformation, so we can speed up the time required for change. This is similarly true regarding some of those major wounds, unhealthy habits, or painful patterns like addiction, exploitation, or selfishness that may exist in our families. With compassion and dedicated effort over time, and with the help of other family members, you can create the healing you desire. One purpose of this book is to provide some communication and group problem-solving tools so that more healing and transformation can be achieved within our families. Of course, there are situations where ultimately the help of a professional counselor or therapist will be required to assist the family to get on track. Yet, we can begin moving the transformation by patiently and persistently applying family activist tools and strategies.

While there are no guarantees that your efforts will result in all your family and friends becoming more caring people or activists, trust that there will be positive outcomes. By pursuing health and transformation, those around you will learn how to take better care of each other, and how to extend this caring beyond the family. Whether it is having a conversation that empowers your niece, enlisting friends to join you at a rally, or facilitating a family gathering that inspires the feeling of love, each act contributes to family well-being, heaven on Earth, and the Great Turning.

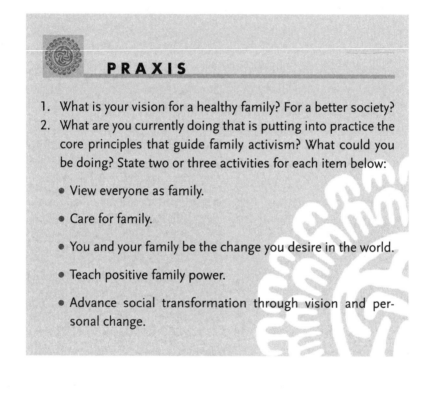

PRAXIS

1. What is your vision for a healthy family? For a better society?
2. What are you currently doing that is putting into practice the core principles that guide family activism? What could you be doing? State two or three activities for each item below:

   • View everyone as family.

   • Care for family.

   • You and your family be the change you desire in the world.

   • Teach positive family power.

   • Advance social transformation through vision and personal change.

3

THE FAMILIA APPROACH

Whether you are eighteen or eighty years old, the parent or child in your family, or even if your closest family is made up of your best friends, you can be a force that nurtures group connection and inspires others to be their best. You can create positive changes for your family and friends, and even develop your own activist communities. To do this, your desire and commitment are essential, and knowledge of the *Familia* Approach will help get you there.

The *Familia* Approach is a way of living so as to teach love and activate the positive power of our families and communities. It includes various principles, tools, and commitments to strengthen our ability to create the change we desire, and to optimize the healing potential of our family and friends.

I call it the *Familia* Approach because it was developed out of my experience of being *familia*. Coming from a Chicano and healer tradition, my family life taught me the core lessons of how to be a social healer and a family activist. Family activism is about healing our society by being more *familia*, by caring for and being responsible for family and community. It is making our communities safe and healthy by being family with all our relations, including our loved ones, neighbors, the people down the street, the people at church, school, soccer, or work, and even the child care providers, bus drivers, and housekeepers. Being *familia* with others is treating them with respect and communicating with them to lift their self-esteem or promote their desire to do good for others. In so doing, we prepare our relations to be more caring and possibly to act in more socially responsible ways as well. So the *Familia* Approach is for all people who want to increase health and healing within their family, community, and society.

The intent of this chapter is to present the five commitments that guide the *Familia* Approach, and then to illustrate their application from the story of my family as we sought to assist each other during my mother's recovery from a stroke.

The Five Commitments that Guide the *Familia* Approach

In the healing tradition of my people, we organize healing knowledge in principles of five, believing that the most powerful medicine involves the interplay of five healing elements or treatments. Given the manner in which our earth is being poisoned and ugly wars are fueling even greater hate, we need radical social healing and transformation. This is why the five commitments have been organized within our traditional medicine wheel, as illustrated on the next page. The more activists and people we can activate to live by these principles, the more we are advancing love, transformation, and the Great Turning.

COMMITMENTS THAT GUIDE

THE FAMILIA APPROACH

1. Teach Love.
2. Be the Change.
3. Co-power Others.
4. Facilitate Connection.
5. Activate Transformation.

Each of the commitments involves a goal and a type of action. The goal of "Teach Love" is love, and the action is teaching. The goal of

The *Familia* Approach
The Guiding Commitments

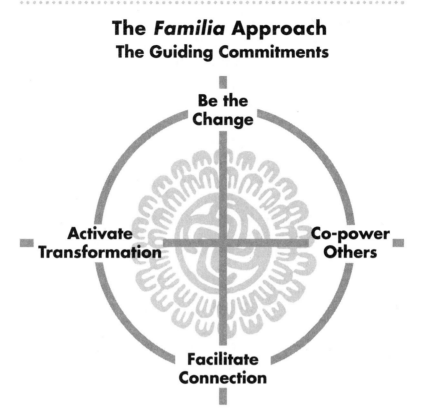

Be the Change

Activate Transformation

Co-power Others

Facilitate Connection

"Be the Change" is change, and the action is "being" through all your thoughts and contacts. The goal of "Co-power Others" is for people to support the empowerment of each other, which is also the action. The goal of "Facilitate Connection" is to connect people with people, and the action is facilitating. The goal of "Activate Transformation" is change and transformation, and the action is the art of activating. Each of these commitments represents a powerful dimension of family activism, and together they comprise a force for radical change and healing needed by many of our families and our U.S. society as a whole.

These principles evolved out of the use of praxis and a community learning process called *razalogia*. As you know, praxis involves thoughtful reflection on one's actions to improve one's practice. For two years I have been involved in a focused praxis period, evaluating almost thirty years of activism toward developing this explanation of family activism. In this effort, I have been using *raza-logia* and interviews. *Razalogia* means "knowledge of and for the people," and involves participants dialoguing to clarify or develop relevant knowledge for community betterment.[1] I interviewed a cross-section of activists from different cultures, age groups, and regions of the country, asking them how they became activists, and whether or how they sought to nurture an activist outlook among their children.

I also reviewed years of documents and memories to identify the principles and tools I have used as a family activist. Once I had an in-depth feel for the multiple tools applied in family activism, I called and interviewed people I respected for their general activism or for their activism regarding family. I systematized this learning into about a dozen strategies which I then shared with various dialogue groups to identify the essential approaches that all family activists should know and develop. The outcome is the *Familia* Approach material that will be presented here. I am now using this model to inform and train community activists seeking to increase family and group power within their target communities.

Living the *Familia* Approach

During the past year, I made a major shift in my activism as Rebeca and I decided to move from our life in the greater San Francisco area to rural southern California to care for my mother. I came with the intention of becoming a companion to my mother, yet quickly discovered we had stepped into an opportunity to experience another dimension of family activism. We are caring for my mother and she for us as we support each other in our life, work, and activism. Because our new living arrangement is full of so many lessons about family activism, I draw examples from this life chapter to illustrate what being a family activist can look like when guided by the *Familia* Approach. First I'll share some of our story.

Last year, Rebeca and I relocated 350 miles to live with my eighty-six-year-old mother, Mama Tita. Mom's stroke left her with some loss of memory and a decrease in physical abilities, and our extended family made a commitment to support the quality of her life in any way we could. Rather than moving her to live with any of us, my brother Marcos and his wife, Robin, initially moved in with her. After almost a year, Rebeca and I saw that Mama Tita needed more attention and that it was beginning to tax my brother's family, which includes two small children. We also felt it was our turn to extend care; consequently, we moved in with her so she could continue to enjoy living in her hometown surrounded by her family and friends.

The idea of moving in with my mom felt adventurous, meaning rife with challenges. We were going to have to resolve the many differences and issues of change when mature adults come to live together. I will mention a few. Mom offered us most of her living area, yet we were accustomed to more space. While Mama Tita and Rebeca love each other, they have several different values and ways of living. Rebeca enjoys a glass of wine at dinner, while my mother feels drinking any alcohol disrespects her. My mother likes to feed others by preparing Mexican food, while Rebeca enjoys a wide variety of dishes.

Within a week of moving in, it was evident that our family meetings needed to start soon. When we finally had a morning to share, I proposed that we meet during breakfast. Everyone agreed. I suggested, "Let's talk first about what we like about living together, what kind of environment we want to create, and then talk about any concerns, feelings, or problems that have been coming up." Given our shared experience with family meetings and planning conversations, we all jumped into the discussion.

I expressed that I felt great that we were together and very grateful to Rebeca and my mom for all they had done to support each other during these changes. I looked forward to strengthening the trust between us so that if any of us had any concerns with each other we would raise them. I cited an example: I see my mother and Rebeca have different views about eating and food. Mother likes to be thrifty and prefers eating leftovers before making new meals, while Rebeca likes to prepare whatever she feels like eating on any particular evening. "I hope we can all talk to each other when we notice these differences."

With the positive tone set, we were able to converse to successfully resolve various concerns. Our cohabitation energy improved considerably during the next month as we continued to meet weekly to plan and develop ways to improve our communications.

Eight months later, the adventure continues, yet I feel I am living heaven on Earth. I have developed the routine of doing movement exercises first thing in the morning with my mother. I am teaching her and reminding myself how to stretch. We typically share breakfast, lunch, and dinner together, which often includes collective food preparation, prayer, and conversation. I grocery shop, she or we do the food preparation, and she insists on doing the cleanup. We also work together to maintain several colorful gardens that provide our daily strawberries, tomatoes, and assorted vegetables. In between, I devote as much time as I can to my consultant work, writing, and maintaining the household.

During this time, we have also enjoyed numerous conversations, sharing circles, and family meetings. My mother better understands my work, and decided to delay her hernia surgery to minimize stress for me as I complete this book. I support her regarding her telephone and prayer activism. Having lost her ability to drive and visit people who need support, her focus now is maintaining the church's prayer network, which includes making telephone calls and devoting time to send prayers to those experiencing difficult times, especially those who have lost a loved one. Periodically, I participate in her prayer sessions or assist her in writing cards for those to whom she wants to send an inspirational message.

Meanwhile, Rebeca and I have been learning about dementia, patience, and more about love. The changes we are experiencing have not just been about improving communication with my mother and with each other, but also with my brothers. Now that we all live in the same vicinity, we are periodically meeting to coordinate support for our mother in a way that is fair to each of us given our multiple commitments, and we are exploring collaboration on several community projects.

While doing all of the above, I keep in mind the commitments of the *Familia* Approach. Over the years they have become so internalized that they are second nature for me. So as I interact with my mother, wife, brothers, their families, or my children from afar, I seek to model love, co-power, foster connection, and activate transformation. Others in my family are doing similarly. So as to provide greater meaning to each of the five commitments, I will be mostly sharing examples of the approaches that Rebeca, Mama Tita, and I have been employing as we have been living together.

Explaining and Illustrating the Five Commitments

Teach Love

Love is core to the vision of the world we desire to see, and to our motivation to serve others and better our world. As family activists, our vision is a society and culture that intentionally seek to become more loving by supporting and respecting each other and our earth. The greatest resource we have to advance this vision is that part of our inherent human nature that is loving. Therefore, our role as activists is to nurture that caring instinct within ourselves and others. We can best do this by modeling caring and love.

Ask most activists to recall the path that led to their social commitment and they often will remember possessing a strong sense of caring, which was transformed into a dedication to justice by an experience that enraged or inspired them to desire change. Then ask them how they developed their caring nature, and most recall being touched and inspired by the loving actions of family members. These experiences shaped their caring spirit. Love is not taught by lecturing, but by modeling and demonstrating love in all that we do. This can be taking time to share conversation, providing assistance to each other, or working extra jobs to financially ensure that our family will have food, clothing, shelter, and the opportunity to grow.

Examples of family activism that model teaching love:

- I seek to make time for conversation with Mama Tita. I listen to her thoughts and encourage her to share feelings, explore her memory, and develop opinions. I do better on some occasions than others, yet I know that I am creating moments of happiness for her while personally learning more about love and patience.

- Mama Tita seeks to relieve me of various household chores so that I have more time for my writing, which she believes will help make our families and world better. So she cuts up my morning fruit salad, makes me an afternoon sandwich, and during those times when I have my office room door closed, tries to buffer me from various visitors who arrive.

- When my young nieces visit, both my mom and I in our own ways seek to nurture them with love. My mother welcomes them with warmth, hugs, and usually their favorite dish, even though given her physical limitations this requires tremendous effort. Asking her about this, she said it's love that gives her the energy to get up in the morning or to coordinate her tired body to make those favorite dishes. Love also helps her smile or do whatever chores she can so as not to burden us with more. My actions with the nieces tend to be more mindful, as I seek to engage these young ones in conversations or activities that teach them about themselves and their responsibility to the family.

- Mama Tita handles each of her telephone conversations in a way that makes the other person feel heard and that models love. Family and church friends call throughout the day, some to check on her and others for a little dose of her loving affection. They will share what is going on in their lives or work, and she will often provide a reflection that validates the good that person is or could be doing.

- Rebeca's current activism includes her working to financially support the family and permit me to use these months to care for my mother and write this book. When she is at home, she prepares meals that are healthy and that she believes my mother and I will enjoy. She also spends a little quality conversation time with my mother while they watch my mother's favorite evening soap opera. Later in this chapter, I will share about the activism Rebeca does at her work.

Be the Change

All the positive values we desire to see in the world, such as fairness, respect, and peace, need to be practiced in our everyday interactions among all our relations. Many activists learned to be caring, courageous, and vocal because they saw these qualities modeled by close family or friends. Therefore family activists live and model the change we want to see through our one-to-one exchanges with others and in the family environment we maintain.

One of our objectives is to develop a family environment that is about peace, respect, and support. This type of family culture nurtures our spirit, supports our growth, and makes life joyful. It also teaches us about the community life we seek to create. The intent of the *Familia* Approach is to guide us in using mindfulness, communication, and group facilitation to create for our family, or any group, this type of atmosphere that encourages dialogue, growth, and development. We create the culture and society we desire by making it happen within our circles of family and friends. Also, in seeking to be fair or proactive within our family relationships, we learn to be the same within our work and public relationships.

Examples of family activism that model being change:

- Believing that our society should take care of our elders and children, Rebeca and I chose to live with my mother despite the challenges of selling our home, moving, and living on a reduced income. We followed my brother Marcos and his wife, who did the same.
- When possible, we have organized special family gatherings in which we have invited aunts, uncles, or cousins who could benefit from the family connection. This year's Father's Day was an example. We invited for dinner one uncle and aunt whose grown-up children live out of state, and another uncle and aunt we wanted to acknowledge for the support they have always shared with all of us. Then we facilitated our dinner conversation so that within the mix of shared stories and laughter there was a real honoring not only for the fathers at the table, but for everyone present, as we genuinely listened to and appreciated each other.

Co-power Others

We co-power when we consciously seek to encourage family and friends as individuals and as family networks to believe in their power and develop the skills to achieve desired results. We want our family and friends to be successful and achieve good for themselves and our communities. This requires their developing self-confidence, social consciousness, and basic skills in problem-solving and critical thinking. Social consciousness involves the capacity to understand our society and world, particularly the forces that undermine our well-being and those that could be employed to improve our world.

Our responsibility to all our relations, young and old, is to strengthen their self-confidence, support their discovery of purpose, and develop their skills for life success, such as goal-setting and focused action. We want as many of our communications as possible to lift people up, to encourage them to actualize their potential to be caring and intelligent people able to affect change in their personal life and the world. Similarly, we encourage social consciousness by engaging family in conversations about what is occurring within our communities, our nation, and the larger world, and what we would like to see occur. We ask questions, tell stories, and listen in order to advance learning that will help us understand our society and ourselves, and support the progress of the Great Turning.

Examples of family activism that model co-powering:

- As I have sought for so many years to make my conversations with others co-powering, it has become a natural way of conversing. Part of my morning movement and prayer ritual includes empowering myself with this intention. Then during most of the day, as I interact with my mother, wife, children, or friends, I listen closely to their needs and challenges and seek to serve by asking questions and providing reflections that enable them to affirm their talents, fuel their positive attitude, and connect more with their power.
- During my morning breakfast conversations with Mama Tita, I scan the paper and then explain the events affecting our community in a way that she will understand. In conversing with her about such issues as the plight of the homeless or the impact of war spending on declining education and human

services, I am also teaching myself how to better explain these issues to others. This is helpful as I share similar conversations with family and friends who visit. At the same time, my mother's commitment to family activism is to weigh my comments and to express her thoughts in return.

- For our recent Thanksgiving dinner, my brother Art and his daughter Andrea prepared a presentation for the family on changes we could make in our homes to become more energy and water efficient. The information shared and conversation that followed were co-powering for all of us, particularly for Art as he received considerable validation for his new business, designing home landscapes that optimize the conservation of water and green values.

- When my young (five and seven years old) nieces visit, I try to have at least five minutes of quality connection with each of them. This usually involves initiating a game or conversation in which I strengthen our bonds through fun, seek to understand their current thoughts or feelings, and leave seeds of ideas or questions for them to consider. All this is intended to help develop, over time, their self-confidence, positive values, and power.

- Meanwhile, Rebeca is very much engaged in similar activism at work. She calls it "positive professionalism." Through her interactions with all her colleagues within the city government, she works to foster a positive feeling about themselves and the work they do. Among support staff, coworkers, and people from other departments, she validates their contributions and encourages their initiative. She does this through one-to-one conversations, and even e-mails, in which she builds relationships, expresses gratitude for assistance, and validates others for their contributions. To inspire the initiative of others she asks strategic questions like, "Ideally, what do you think would be best?" or "How could we make a difference?" Her intent is to co-power others to enjoy their work and contribute their best toward developing a positive work environment and serving the city. By the number of compliments she receives, it's evident that she is making a difference.

Facilitate Connection

People need to be brought together to connect and to make good things happen. When people connect they establish the conditions that support meaningful conversations that can increase learning and power for all involved. Family activists do what is needed to make every family gathering an opportunity to deepen connection, express love, and teach skills for communication, organizing, and problem solving. This involves developing skills to facilitate or "to make easy" conversations or gatherings that bring family and friends together to have fun or to plan meaningful projects. Both activities can be facilitated so the end result increases caring and life-changing action. The *Familia* Approach utilizes such tools and traditions as doing *conocimiento*[2]—sharing conversation with each other—councils, ceremonies, and unity circles for celebration, fun, planning, or transformative work.

Examples of family activism that model facilitating connection:

- After I facilitated the first family meetings around our new family arrangement, Rebeca or Mama Tita would call for family conversations whenever they felt necessary. Given our years of experience with meetings, we organically share the responsibilities of facilitating and making the conversations successful.

- Together, Rebeca, Mama Tita, and I have initiated, organized, or facilitated a series of semi-regular family events. These have mostly been Sunday gatherings where my brothers and their families join us for lunch. It takes all three of us to organize the house and coordinate the meal, yet it's always worth it to enjoy being *familia*. My mother feels happy that the family is together, we genuinely enjoy being together, and there is always great potential for an interesting conversation or the development of a new plan. In these gatherings, everyone contributes in different ways. There are talkers, listeners, and facilitators, and everyone seems to do some of each. Periodically I informally serve as facilitator because the family trusts the way I manage conversations so everyone is heard and resolutions are achieved, yet this has become less necessary given the skills everyone has developed for respectful communication.

- At times I have scheduled activist or work meetings at the house. With my mom's help, we create a *familia* type environment for our guests (organizers or community educators) where we can deepen our connections and get into meaningful learning and planning conversations about our work. While my mother's natural inclination would be to disappear, feeling intimidated by the "intelligent" people visiting her home, I try to have her accept that she is brilliant regarding families and communities, and that she has just as much to teach us as we might be able to offer her. Usually, on the principle of being a good host, she agrees to join us to offer a short welcome.

- Initiating conversations for connecting often leads to planning and collaboration. As we connect and hear each other's challenges we often desire to find resolutions. In this way, connecting conversations have led to planning regarding necessary repairs to my mother's home or ways to support my brother Art's new business or wedding plans.

Activate Transformation

The goals of family activism include healthy families, good relationships, and transformative change. This involves providing ongoing support, inspiration, and education to develop more loving and responsible families, and then engaging our families in the work of creating social change.

Activating transformation is possibly the most advanced form of family activism, and I am still learning about it. In activating transformation, we are mindfully taking the sequential actions that can lead to or inspire others to participate in individual and social change. It's supporting the development of others, so that an individual can move from being directionless to becoming purposeful, or a family can shift from focusing on material success to valuing community service. It can be getting neighbors to a political rally or working with family and friends to elect a progressive candidate.

Family activists have the long-term picture in mind. Consequently, they patiently work toward changing the prejudicial attitude of a

Family activism nurtures confidence, social awareness, and connection.
Marcos makes community demonstrations part of his children's experience.

friend, developing the spirit of community service among the family youth, or fostering a sense of power among neighbors so they can act together to ensure a safer neighborhood or develop programs to support the success of their children. Family activists know that achieving these goals often involves a multiplicity of mutually supportive actions, and they invest in many one-to-one conversations over time to nurture confidence, social awareness, and connection, trusting that ultimately they can lead to collaborative community actions.

Examples of family activism that model activating or supporting transformation:

- As I worked on this book in my new community, I reached out to various people to talk over the ideas and tools presented here. My goals were: (1) to invite feedback to help strengthen the clarity of the ideas, (2) to begin developing my new community of support, and (3) to activate other people to consider a greater use of the tools of family activism. Some of these people have already become collaborators in applying these tools and strategies toward empowering their local communities. In turn, I have learned new lessons as their questions and feedback have identified areas that I still need to learn about.

- I have also begun my process of neighborhood community building. Whenever I see a neighbor and have a moment, I go over to introduce myself. I'm creating a telephone roster for my new neighborhood and developing the relationships that will make this street feel like home. At present, I have no strategic objectives in mind for our street, yet as we get to know each other, the objectives will evolve. Maybe we'll organize street parties to strengthen our connection, become more available to support each other during emergencies, or maybe some of us will join together to address local concerns.

- As my brother Marcos is more directly involved in community empowerment and policy change, he calls to make certain we are aware of strategic public hearings or protests where our presence counts. Consequently, we have made several protest rallies an outing for family and friends.

- Recently, one of my daughters requested to live with us so she can save money for school, then so did one of her friends, and now also my nephew, who has secured a part-time position as a youth organizer. These young people are still in the formative years of developing a career that can sustain them, and they are all contributors to social change or community welfare. All of us, including my mother, wife, brothers, and the young people, developed a plan to optimize our resources so that we can look after Mama Tita, financially support the young people in their evolving careers and activism, and support each other in achieving our goals.

The purpose of the five commitments is to focus our energies as family activists and provide a guiding structure for the *Familia* Approach. The next chapter offers a sense of the family transformation that can occur through applying this method.

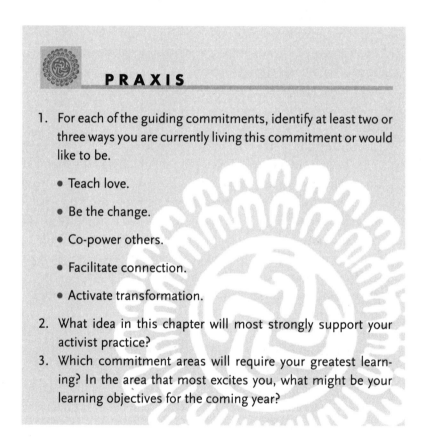

PRAXIS

1. For each of the guiding commitments, identify at least two or three ways you are currently living this commitment or would like to be.

   - Teach love.

   - Be the change.

   - Co-power others.

   - Facilitate connection.

   - Activate transformation.

2. What idea in this chapter will most strongly support your activist practice?

3. Which commitment areas will require your greatest learning? In the area that most excites you, what might be your learning objectives for the coming year?

4

FAMILY ACTIVISM AND
TRANSFORMATION

The most powerful tools to advance the well-being of our relationships, families, and communities are our love and the vision we develop of what is possible. We can create relationships of powerful mutual support. We can transform family life from complacent disconnection to purposeful enthusiasm that inspires change. We can develop communities to become a movement for cultural transformation and corporate accountability.

The prior chapters spoke to the philosophy of family activism, key definitions, guiding principles, and the commitments that comprise the *Familia* Approach. Before I present the actual tools involved in my approach to family activism, I want to introduce a vision of possibility by sharing the story of how family activism contributed to the transformation of my family. Not that we have become a model of the ultimate caring family, yet we were able to move from a state of dysfunction to become a true *familia*, taking good care of each other while contributing much love to our multiple communities.

Besides providing a vision of what ongoing family transformation can look like, our story also begins to illustrate the interplay of the tools fundamental to the *Familia* Approach to family activism, such as *conocimiento*, facilitation, co-powering, and optimizing the healing qualities of the family council. I share our story to possibly awaken for you a vision for your family or community, and to provide a sense of the realities and benefits involved in the activism of change that begins with our own families.

Organizing Our First Council

As activists, one objective we have is to develop family traditions and skills for meaningful meetings that encourage love and enable us to better support each other.

Whether it's called a family meeting or a council, this is a practice that provides members the opportunity to connect, converse, and plan, while empowering the family overall. For many, "council" conveys the full significance of a meeting that is not a time for lectures by dad or mom, but an interactive process that invites everyone to address group concerns. All are invited to speak, and all have the responsibility to listen.

Initiating our council tradition assisted my family to move from a place of avoidance, denial, and dysfunction. The council served to facilitate major healing, foster closer relationships, and create a family culture of mutual support. It has enabled us to experience love and collaboration, and to create energy to assist others and serve our communities. It was not a tradition that was systematically taught to us; we had to learn and evolve the practice so that it could serve our family. As you read our story, consider how the council worked for us and how it might be of value for your family.

The story of our family council tradition began years ago when a major conflict surfaced between siblings, followed by family denial of the problem, and deteriorating relationships.

Like many families, mine brought together different traditions and histories. My mother's family actively shared conversation and expressed feelings. When we joined together there was often laughter, hugs, and tears. In contrast, my father's family included talented storytellers, but there was rigidity about sharing feelings and minimal exchange of conversation. The result was that our father dominated group conversation. His communication practice was to have the first word, the last word, and most of the words in between. If we had concerns involving feelings, we typically spoke with our mother.

A couple of years after moving 400 miles from home to work and study, I was touring the Southwest assisting various groups in community problem-solving when I made a visit to my family for badly needed personal nurturance. Instead, I discovered that a major unspoken secret was beginning to tear the family apart. Although it pained me, it also frustrated me because I felt that I knew what my family needed, yet I lived so far away. We needed to reconnect with each other, converse, and initiate a family council. Inspired by this vision, I asked my girlfriend, Rebeca, to help me develop a plan.

First, I persuaded my father to support me in convening a family meeting that I said was necessary for my studies. This was true in part, as I saw creating healthy families as the purpose of my work. To create the opportunity for a fresh type of family gathering, we invited everyone to our home in Oakland, California, for Thanksgiving.

When the day arrived, I was disappointed that two of my brothers who were chiefly involved in the conflict, Jack and Marcos, did not attend, despite my personal invitation to each. However, we continued with the plan. I opened our gathering explaining that my work involved teaching families how to use the council to maintain family connection, and the purpose of this meeting was to reconnect and explore ways to become a healthier family. I asked that we begin with a *conocimiento* (getting to know each other) practice in which each person would share three positive qualities they brought to our family.

The group accepted the plan. One by one, each spoke. All progressed well until it was Mom's turn to speak. She broke down crying, uttering that she couldn't think of any positive personal qualities. My father immediately blasted her, "What's wrong with you? You know that it's you that keeps this family together." My mother, who appeared somewhat shocked, responded, "You have never said that before." To which my father looked to all of us saying, "I don't know what's wrong with your mother." I asked my father if he could repeat what my mother had just said. He asserted, "I don't have to tell her what she knows." My brother then offered his reflection, saying, "But, Dad, she says you've never told her what she does for our family. Maybe you should tell her now?"

An insight came to mind with this exchange. I realized how infrequently we as family members acknowledged each other's positive qualities or contributions. Consequently, I asked everyone if we could shift our plan and focus now on sharing the positive qualities we saw in each other. I hung easel paper on the wall and wrote the name of each family member, including my two absent brothers. Then we brainstormed while I listed the positive qualities we saw in each person. Our session was truly inspiring. It was the first time we had ever validated what we appreciated in each other. Both our parents glowed as they heard the admirable traits their children and Rebeca saw in them.

Feeling our connection and positive energy, I asked that we share what we could do to become a healthier family. The group brainstormed their ideas and I listed them. When my turn came, I asked whether, given our desire for more communication and openness, I could raise a concern. I then shared, "I feel we need to talk about the fact that we all know Jack is gay, because not talking about it is tearing our family apart."

My dad's immediate reaction was anger and control: "There's nothing to talk about. Your brother is sick. We can only pray for him." My mother started to cry again, eventually revealing that she felt she was to blame because long ago she had prayed for a daughter. The dialogue intensified. My youngest brother, Art, and I told my mother she was not responsible for Jack's sexual orientation because her prayers were not the cause. Art, who was greatly respected by our father for his manliness and physical strength, then stunned everyone when he said that he respected Jack for his courage in being himself. My father was shocked.

In the conversation that ensued, we shared both our love for Jack and our various perspectives about gays. There was no major shift in the view of our parents at this time, yet we did open the wound that had been festering. For the first time we were openly recognizing his gay identity, the division it had created between him and our brother Marcos, and how their conflict was affecting all of us. Marcos, who now is a strong advocate for gay rights, at the time strongly felt that Jack's sexual orientation was an embarrassment to the family and refused to even be in the same room with him. As the meeting drew to a close, we all agreed to continue scheduling councils until we brought the whole family together.

With me living in Northern California and my family in Southern California, the best we could do was to schedule three gatherings a

My family in 1982: Marcos, Andrea, Roberto, Jack, Dad, Mom, and Art

year. Over the next couple of years, first one and then the other brother participated, and finally we were all able to join together. Marcos came to realize the irrationality of his homophobia. He apologized for his behavior, extended his appreciation for our council efforts, and became not only an active ally to the gay community, but a person we are proud of for his deep commitment to community service.

Using the council, we developed stronger bonds of connection and mutual support. Although my father still dominated the dinner conversation, on those occasions designated as council time, he honored the practice of every person having an allotted time to speak. To reinforce this process, I introduced the tradition of the talking stick, which comes from our indigenous culture. Whoever holds the stick has the "word," or the authority to speak, and is responsible to speak from the heart and to voice truth. During that time, everyone else is responsible to listen.

My father struggled with this tradition because it meant he had to relinquish control, yet as he saw how we listened, his monologues became shorter and his words more meaningful. Several years later, my father experienced a debilitating stroke, and we made use of the council to plan and coordinate support for him and my mother. Six months later, he died. The death of one's parent is always difficult, yet we realized that we had much to be grateful for. Our father had sought to be the best person that he could be, and his dedication contributed to shaping our lives. We were glad that our evolving tradition of the council had affected his life positively, and that he had enjoyed a number of beautiful family conversations before his passing. Recognizing the value of the family council, we expanded the practice to develop our family retreat tradition.

The Family Retreat

During the fifteen years following my father's death, our family has expanded and moved to different parts of the country. Still, our council tradition has evolved and deepened.

At one of our early councils, the idea surfaced of organizing a weeklong retreat at the beach. Jack was now more fully accepted by the family, yet the idea of participating in that much family time seemed too much for him, so he was reluctant to commit. As our plans proceeded, Jack decided that he would join us for a day's visit, but he enjoyed himself so much that he stayed for the remainder of the week. As a result of this first family retreat, we established a reunion tradition that we maintained and refined over the next dozen years.

Certain practices became standard at these reunions. The main idea was to include the entire family, which expanded to Jack's partner, other people's prospective partners, in-laws, and godchildren. Second, the first evening was dedicated to a family meeting to develop our agenda for the week. One by one, everyone from the youngest to the oldest would share their expectations for the reunion, which my daughter would list on the easel paper taped to the wall. The expectations varied from time for personal reading and sleeping to group sand castle making, bike riding, and family sessions. Building on these wishes, and the practice of rotating assignments for meal preparation, we developed a general schedule. It included ample free time, time for various activities, a couple of family sharing sessions to nurture our connection, and usually a council for the brothers to address issues regarding care for our mother.

For most of us, it was the family sharing gatherings, our "family circles," that were the most inspiring. We met specifically to do *conocimiento*, or listening and catching up with each other. Sometimes these were scheduled after a meal or for a campfire evening. We would open the family circle by deciding on the *conocimiento* topic, which was most often "share your goals and challenges for the coming year." To this, a youngster might add, "and share your most embarrassing experience." As the convener, I often began with my sharing and then offered the talking stick to whomever was to my left. After each person spoke, the stick was passed again, giving every person, young and old, a turn sharing goals, challenges, and life stories.

During this sharing, members not only updated the family on their plans, but also shared appreciation to others for their support, or put forth requests for assistance for the coming year. A tissue box often came out during the first round as tears of good emotion flowed. If there was time, we engaged in another sharing round so participants could express their feelings about or response to any issue that had come up. Often we shared feelings of love, compassion, and pride that genuinely nurtured the soul. For all of us, the sharing in these family circles made love real. We would see it in the courage of one person telling a difficult truth, a child sharing his or her thoughts, or the exchange of heartfelt feelings between members.

Everyone in our family has stories of how they applied skills learned in our councils to convene meetings within their school, job, or community service arenas, including my mother. Tired of hearing the complaints of her cafeteria coworkers, she suggested a council meeting so everyone could share their concerns and the group could establish priorities and then decide what to do. In-laws and friends who have participated in our councils have also reported back that they took the practice to their own families to nurture connection and to solve problems they were facing.

Developing Our Family Vision

Thirty years after our first council, my mother, my brothers, and our families continue to get together for at least two gatherings each year. Now, we meet not so much to plan as to keep each other current. We meet to hear each other's stories, celebrate victories, and discover how we can support or collaborate with each other. Because of the hectic realities of our lives and our geographic spread, which is now from California to New York, not everyone can always attend, so we use the Internet and telephone to maintain the link with those not able to be physically present.

I had been thinking about our next Thanksgiving and Christmas gatherings because for the first time in several years most of the family would be present for both holidays. The idea arose to enlist the group to develop a family mission statement. While we all share a commitment to support each other and serve the larger community, I thought it would be even more powerful if we made our family mission explicit.

We scheduled our family circle to follow Thanksgiving dinner. I introduced the idea of developing a family mission statement, and proposed that our *conocimiento* question be to share what we each viewed as the purpose of our family. There was immediate resistance. First, several members thought my request was "too heady," then my younger daughter, Cheli, commented that our circle sharing had become boring. The energy of the group suddenly became tense as this young family member questioned a practice that had become core to our family. She quickly elaborated that it would be more fun if we could vary how we do our circle by holding conversations in pairs, doing skits, or making collages. Our energy quickly shifted as we all acknowledged that her recommendation was to enliven our tradition.

The new ideas resonated, and we made some quick decisions. For that day, the theme of our sharing would be, "What's important in my life and what is my commitment to the family?" Then, for our Christmas family circle, Cheli was asked to decide on our sharing process and facilitate our council. We then resumed our traditional way of sharing.

As usual, I was prepared to take notes when members shared about their commitments to the family. As with many prior family sessions, I was inspired to hear everyone's thoughts and feelings, from the youngest to eldest. My excitement continued as I consolidated the lists of commitments generated by our circle and imagined the rich follow-up conversations we could have about them. The family commitments included:

- Help each other grow.
- Support the family connection.
- Extend support to each other.
- Enjoy sharing family time.
- Advance *porvida* love within family and community.

Like a kid, I enthusiastically waited for Christmas. With Cheli slated to facilitate, we were beginning to pass the tradition on to the younger generation, and I looked forward to a new *conocimiento* experience. Given logistical issues like children's bedtime and other family needs, we decided to share Christmas Eve dinner together, followed by the first part of our family sharing circle, with the second part to occur the following morning after breakfast and our exchange of gifts.

After Christmas Eve dinner, Cheli asked that we all gather in the living room. In the middle of the floor were piled more than four dozen magazines and lots of art supplies, including poster board, cork board, pins, glue, and scissors. Her instructions were simple: (1) Make a collage representing your personal vision and hopes for the coming year, and (2) on the large easel paper titled *Familia* Vision, attach any images reflecting vision and hopes you have for the family. That night we were to make our collages, comprised of various images we drew or took from the magazines, and the following morning after opening presents, we would share about them.

Everyone got creative, from the three-year-old niece to all her aunts and uncles. Soon the entire living room floor was blanketed with cut or torn images as family members exchanged and helped each other find particular illustrations. While we were in the middle of all this fun, the doorbell rang. We had visitors! A half dozen high

Making our collages.

school and college-age cousins looking for a party walked in. They were invited to participate, and most did. Within the hour there were collages decorating the walls, strong feelings of love, and each of us with insights discovered through the exercise.

The next day's *conocimiento* circle was revealing. Each person shared about their collage and about the images they had placed on the *Familia* Vision poster. The colorful imagery selected by each person proved more insightful than most of us would have imagined, and many of us discovered more about our desires than we had been aware of before. I realized how important it was for me to grow a garden this year, my daughter revealed her desire to attend photography school, one brother recognized his commitment to health, and another to finally get married. Along with our various personal revelations, many of us expressed ways we could support and collaborate with each other.

Because some family members were unable to attend the second session, we decided to integrate their sharing at the next opportunity. I asked to serve as the caretaker of the *Familia* Vision poster until our next meeting. Each of the images and the accompanying statements were inspirational. There was the image of a young

Sharing our collages and our visions and hopes for the future.

woman of color that said "Grow Leaders" next to the image of a protestor marching with a sign saying "March for Women's Lives." In the center was a picture of a family gathering spilling out into the front yard of a house, bringing to mind my wish to more actively extend our *familia* spirit to our neighbors. There was also a picture of two cuddling chimpanzees, which Cheli said was to remind us to be loving.

Family councils are special meetings organized to address family needs and advance the tradition of being *familia*, caring for each other and our community. Initially, our councils were designed to support necessary healing and to plan on behalf of the family. In many ways, those early councils taught us how to dialogue and work as a group. Later, our purpose became to stay current with each other, inspire each other, and discover ways to support one another. As one of my daughters explains to others, "We do council to share love."

Using the Council to Become More *Familia*

To be *familia* is to live in connection with and support those we love. We learn connection within our families, and this is what we want for our society as well. With increased connection, people are more available to understand and support each other. There is greater caring and empathy, and less abuse and violence. More people work for the common good, and fewer are focused solely on selfish wants.

While the quality of family depends on the multiple one-to-one interactions that occur among members, it is essential to experience and learn how to be family as a group. We need to be able to join together and hear all voices, not merely the oldest, loudest, or male ones. We need to invite the words of each person and hear them in the spirit of understanding and willingness to support. The council provides us the opportunity to learn and do this type of sharing to become more "family."

Before our first council, my family did not have gatherings that fostered this type of practice. For many years when my father worked away from home, my mother would serve the kids dinner while she continued working in the kitchen. Finally, when I was thirteen years old, we moved so that our father could regularly live with us. This is when our family first began eating dinner together, yet our mealtimes were often tense as my dad would predominantly speak, argue, or suppress arguments. While Dad was a great storyteller and there were moments of quality time together, it was frustrating to hold back my thoughts and be unable to build ideas through conversation.

I have learned that the majority of families do not have a tradition of meaningful meetings or conversations. Without a tradition that supports genuine dialogue, we lose the opportunity to fully feel and build on our connection, and develop our family as a source for learning and joy.

I initiated the council within my family because the connection we had was deteriorating, the togetherness we had was being lost. I was motivated to improve our relationships because the thought of being disconnected was painful. Without family togetherness, where would I find joy or nurture my purpose?

Initiating the first council, I had several things going for me. I was the oldest son, I was committed to advancing the well-being of my family, and I knew the basics required for successful meetings—a designated facilitator, a stated purpose, a clarified process, and active supporters.

Securing my father's consent for me to be the facilitator was crucial. I explained to him that as the facilitator I was responsible to: (1) guide the meeting according to a plan that we would all agree upon; (2) ensure that everyone was heard during the meeting; and (3) make sure that we accomplished our goals. He agreed, but in addition, before the meeting, I secured commitments from my girlfriend and youngest brother to support me in getting our family to a better place by actively participating. When the gathering began, I opened by clarifying our purpose and explaining our proposed process. Once we began, I minimized my own talking to create the opportunity for others to speak, while periodically helping keep participants focused and validating our accomplishments.

Despite the difficult and challenging moments we experienced during that first meeting, everyone recognized its value, and an important new tradition was born. In my view, the council facilitated miracles for my family. Attitudes shifted that ultimately opened us to accept our differences. My brothers and I began to learn what it means to be an ally to one's brothers, and to gay men. We began being family in new ways that empowered us with greater self-confidence, vision, and skills. Given the healing and change we experienced, most of us began seeing the possibilities for change in other arenas in our lives, and in our community work and activism.

Can this process be replicated within other families? Absolutely! I desired to make this medicine possible for others, so when I subsequently taught university courses on community organizing, a core assignment was to organize a family meeting. Repeatedly, students resisted, saying they were studying how to organize community, not family. I countered with several points:

- Once you organize a family meeting, a community meeting is much easier.
- Social change takes time, so begin working with your family so they will become your support in the future.
- If you really want to change the world, it often begins with your family.

Because it was a class requirement, the students would organize a council, mostly with family, yet sometimes with roommates or others they considered family. Invariably, they discovered the power of councils for making their family or constellation of friends more connected and mutually supportive.

We also learned that some families are not ready to engage in respectful communication, yet by trying we learn from our experience, we often plant seeds of possibilities for later, and, most important, we know that we tried. Whenever anyone has tried to organize a council there have been positive outcomes—though maybe not the ones we immediately desired. There has always been personal growth, and maybe the beginning shifts of attitude or growth for others as well. This is how transformation begins.

The chapters that follow explore various wisdom points and skills to assist you in developing your family and facilitating your own councils.

PRAXIS

1. What has been your history of being a healthy family, communicating with each other, and sharing respect and support? What changes would you like to see in yourself or your family that would make life richer for you and for your family members? Note a couple of changes you would like to see in yourself and your family. Keep these in mind as you explore the following chapters on tools for family activism.
2. What are your learnings, insights, or feelings from my family experience? How might you be able to use these insights to support the development of your family?
3. Initially, organizing a family council may feel impossible. The following chapters are intended to provide tools and illustrations of how I and others have used these tools to foster caring and joyful families. While reading them, note in your journal those you wish to develop or apply with your family, your friends, or your other groups such as church, school, or work.

PART II
TOOLS FOR FAMILY POWER

We need a revolution in our approach to education, to
empower ourselves and our children to think, to question, and
to dare to act. You can set an example. Be a teacher and
student; inspire everyone around you through your example.

— JOHN PERKINS, *CONFESSISONS OF
AN ECONOMIC HIT MAN*[1]

If you want a healthy and nurturing family, and successful and
productive children, you must commit yourself to acquiring
the insight and skills necessary to live the values that you
know in your heart are so important.

— DR. PHIL McGRAW, *FAMILY FIRST*[2]

5

GETTING YOUR ACT TOGETHER

T o be a successful family activist and create the change we desire
in the world requires preparation and grounding. This involves
connecting with what nurtures your spirit and energy. It involves
living with integrity, health, and the feeling of success in fulfilling
your goals and objectives. It also involves lasting the distance by living with balance so that you never give up your vision and continue
inspiring others to be their best. To sustain this effort we must prepare ourselves for a life of personal joy and service.

The success I live today I credit to a combination of good fortune,
the connection I made to my spirit, and preparation. I was fortunate
to have had caring people and experiences that pointed me in the
right direction and taught me that life success requires ongoing
learning. Interestingly, that which we do to prepare ourselves for
personal success or to be effective family activists also primes us to
be better supporters and teachers for our family and friends as well.

For this preparation, I advise connecting with your spirit, knowing your *porvida* essence, deepening your understanding of purpose, and clarifying your plan for success.

Make the Spirit Connection

Most of the time, caring for family and friends can be joyful, yet
there are moments and sometimes periods when you may feel
totally overwhelmed with personal challenges that just don't seem
to stop. These are times when you may ask, "Why me, and what am

I to do?" Maybe you lost your job, the family car requires expensive repair, there isn't enough money to pay the bills, or a relationship is ending. Or maybe it's merely everyday life getting messy—you have a work deadline, you're trying to get out of the house, and the kids spill juice all over the kitchen floor. Life happens. So what do you do to remain grounded in your activist vision and purpose?

For me, the best way to stay on course and inspired is to reconnect with spirit, purpose, and love. Early on your path it is wise to clarify what inspires you, so that you can develop those practices that nurture your spirit, make living your purpose joyful, and connect you with your power.

While I was raised within a church community, I consider myself spiritual rather than religious. I believe that life is a beautiful miracle created by God, or the universe, and that my inner being is spirit. I also feel that I am a spirit on a human journey, so when I connect with my spirit I feel more whole, energized, creative, joyful, and able to address my challenges. I am frequently asked how I arrived at this place, and my response is that my path led me to these understandings. For you it will be different, so find your way to connect with spirit and then develop your own practices for nurturing the reconnection.

We all have or are developing our own stories about seeking and making connection with spirit, or deciding whether to believe in God or spirit. Some of us evolved our connection in the course of our religious upbringing, and some in their adult pursuit of spirit through different traditions. Others unexpectedly connect with spirit during a life crisis. If you have made your spirit connection, that's great; if you haven't, maybe it's time to create the opportunity for this to occur. If your exploration has led you to believe there is no spirit, then determine what it is that inspires you to love, feel joy, or want to make the world better. The point I'm making is that our personal preparation begins with clarifying what it is that inspires joy and the desire to serve.

I grew up in a Latino Methodist church and came to love the experience of family and community that occurred every Sunday. The church regulars would greet me and each other with hugs and good words, and the love that flowed made me feel the presence of spirit.

I also loved the feeling of confidence that came from knowing that God was present in my life. Yet it wasn't until my adult life during my early thirties that I actually came to experience meeting and connecting with my spirit. It occurred at a sweat lodge ceremony during which my spirit transcended my body—I found myself simultaneously experiencing my spirit above the lodge and my body in the intense heat within the lodge—while my consciousness was able to admire the courage within both dimensions of myself. Since then, I have only felt that profound degree of connection with spirit a few more times, yet having had that deep encounter has made spirit as real as my heartbeat. Now I can more easily maintain the relationship, particularly as I have developed a life style that permits me to renew this connection every day.

Every morning, I do my movement prayer, which involves movements similar to tai chi that activate my circulatory, nervous, and vital energy systems. As I do these movements, I offer prayers to the four directions. This ritual wakes up my body, gets me into a feeling of gratitude, and prepares me to approach the day as a "mover of love." Later in the day, with every meal I extend my thanks to the universe, and if I am in the company of family, friends, or work associates, I invite everyone to share a few words to the Creator before eating. If I need to reconnect with spirit or my purpose during the day, I can go to one of a number of altar or inspiration spaces I have created around the house. I can go to my bedroom, which has been decorated with photos and mementos of family and friends who inspire my life. I can go out to those places in our garden that remind me of the beauty that surrounds us. Or I can decide that later in the day I will take a jog or walk for body and spirit.

Having evolved these rituals and practices, it is easier to remain optimistic and resourceful throughout the day. Challenges that arise are consciously reframed as opportunities to access my intelligence or trust my ability to make a difference. If greater support is needed, I ask the Creator or the spirit of my grandmother for assistance, call my wife to tell her I love her, call a friend to request the opportunity to talk, or just go to one of my sacred places for a short break.

I am able to stay on course because I have invested the time to connect with my spirit and develop rituals that help me. This is what each of us has to do for ourselves. Some of us have a religious tradition we can draw upon to aid us in this discovery process, and others do not. Those who don't may not have far to go to find cues to assist them on their path. Entering the spirituality section of your local bookstore with a sincere attitude of exploration may be all that you need to uncover your next steps on this journey. As you enter, asking God or Creator for guidance may assist you in this search. A particularly good book for activists is *The Spiritual Activist*, by Claudia Horwitz, which shows readers how to use mindfulness, ritual, silence, and happenings in everyday life to connect with their spirit.[1] Again, if spiritual practice is not your choice, then use whatever method you are comfortable with to connect with the values, ideas, or energy that inspire and motivate you.

The activist preparation of connecting with spirit is sometimes called grounding, because you are fortifying your connection with that which nurtures you, like a tree that drives its roots deeper into the ground to ensure its sustenance. This includes not only connecting with spirit, but also understanding our *porvida* essence, connecting with our inherent drive to manifest life and love, and deepening awareness of our personal life purpose.

Know You Are *Porvida*

Your essential spirit or energy force is for life and love. You are *porvida*! For many this is a radical idea because we have been taught otherwise, yet once recognized it becomes common sense and connects us with our power.

Like millions of people over the generations, I grew up receiving messages of self-depreciation from church and school. As a youngster, I heard from the Christian ministers, "We are all born sinful." When I started school, the prominent message directed to me and everyone else who looked Mexican was, "You aren't smart enough."

Fortunately, I received another message also. Despite the challenges my mother and grandmother experienced, they showed me absolute love. In all the ways they treated me, and others, they communicated their belief that all people are good, intelligent, full of potential, and worthy of love. I couldn't express it in words, yet I knew my soul at the core of my being was *porvida*, for life.

Knowing and living *porvida* makes my life rich with purpose and fulfillment. I know I am capable of being more loving because that is my human nature. I know I can always be a better person, so I work at it. As I succeed I feel joy because I am living my purpose and developing my potential. It also helps knowing that others are also inherently *porvida*. Accepting this, I seek to see the goodness in others and support their potential. And I envision what we can accomplish together to create a movement in which families and communities live compassion, peace, and service. If I were to see myself and others otherwise, as selfish and sinful, then I would be greatly diminishing my power, their goodness, and the potential we have together.

Recognizing that our human nature is *porvida* is the most important understanding we can reach. When we accept this truth, our power soars. We are all uniquely different, yet upon recognizing our *porvida* nature we feel connected to our spirit, connected to each other, and confident in our power. We recognize our purpose, know what needs to be done, and feel a desire to make it happen.

We are not inherently bad or sinful; we are beings full of love potential just needing to transcend our immaturity. The immature side of our character is fearful, insecure, self-centered, and selfish. Because of our immaturity, we humans have often not yet learned how to nurture our loving essence. Fearful of not getting what we need to survive, many of us become directed to care solely for ourselves. However, with a right combination of love, support, and insight, we can develop our *porvida* loving nature, and realize our essential purpose to become better able to live love.

This knowledge is not new. It has been expressed throughout our human history by such great teachers of spirit as Jesus Christ, Buddha, Mohammad, and Quetzalcoatl.[2] But too often the message of the teachers has been compromised by the followers and institutions that came later, and we lose sight of the fundamental message that we are all part of the miracle of life. We are all part of the goodness of God, with the responsibility to evolve our ability to love.

Our challenge is to shake off the myths we have learned that negate our loving nature, and learn to draw forth the goodness that resides in ourselves and others. This is our fundamental human purpose—to evolve our *porvida* nature and permit the God force or the human potential within us to blossom.

Given my growing experience as a gardener, I believe the story of a corn kernel can provide us insight about our human potential. Take a kernel in your hand, and recognize that this seed has essence and potential. With the proper conditions of sunshine, well-aerated soil, and sufficient water, the life force within this seed can awaken and manifest its essence—to live and grow. It becomes a seedling and, growing in accordance to its purpose, becomes a tall cornstalk that will contribute back to life. With nurturance it can generate several ears of corn, each with hundreds of new kernels that can feed people or animals or birth new plants.

The life essence of the corn kernel is to live, grow, and contribute to life. Similarly, our human essence is to live, grow, evolve our human potential, and contribute back to life. How we mature and what we contribute in life is based on the nurturance we receive, and ultimately how we decide to view ourselves and grow our potential. Whether our lives have been full of negating or validating messages, we can choose to recognize our *porvida* essence, own our purpose, and advance the positive.

When we accept and nurture our life-affirming essence, we become more able to advance love and change. We can develop our maturity with greater purpose and creativity, and nurture our young ones to know their *porvida* spirit. As activists, as people desiring a better world, our power is exponentially greater when we accept our *porvida* nature and live accordingly.

Discovering and Evolving Purpose

Discovering our purpose is essential, and when we can serve another in making this discovery we have made a tremendous contribution to humankind. The story of my early adventure with my *Tia* Fina that I shared in the introduction, and my subsequent development, illustrate this.

Poster by Andrea Vargas-Mendoza for the California Association of Bilingual Educators (CABE) 2003 statewide conference.

We are here to develop our humanity, evolve our spirit, enjoy and contribute back to life.

As I grew up and accumulated new experiences, my purpose became more refined, yet always at the core has been a commitment to help create a better world. This purpose has guided my life and led me to make contributions that have influenced many other lives. I cofounded two family counseling centers, which have served thousands of families over the past thirty years, taught at several universities preparing hundreds of students to be more committed social activists, and provided consultant and training services to scores of organizations throughout the country. I have enjoyed it all because I know I am living my purpose.

I am grateful to my grandmother and mother, who were consistent in living love and from whom I absorbed important values. Similarly, I extend appreciation to my auntie who in that moment of my readiness heard, validated, and inspired me to go within and discover my purpose. That same insight might have surfaced the next day, or maybe much later, yet it happened then because of her love. In her listening and responding with respect and encouragement, I see she was a family activist. This illustrates that among our responsibilities as family activists, it is most vital that we treat others with respect, make them feel worthy, and ask questions that help connect them with their purpose.

Living Your Purpose

Life is all interconnected. Animal and plant, soil and sky, streams and hills, all are part of the miracle of life. Within this miracle our human purpose is to support the evolution of life, beginning with ourselves. We are here to develop our humanity, evolve our spirit, enjoy and contribute back to life. We enhance our power to do all this when we recognize our relationship to life and know our purpose. Vital to discovering and living this way is to periodically ask yourself, "Am I on purpose?"

As youngsters many of us grew up wondering: What is my purpose? Why am I alive? What am I supposed to be doing with my life? Unfortunately, we usually do not have guides to help us find answers. When we did hear from adults, it was typically questions like: What are you going to be when you grow up? What career are you going to pursue? Important questions, yet not ones that help us connect with our deeper purpose, our character, and our spirit.

Besides our core *porvida* mission to evolve our ability to love, we each have a unique purpose that we must discover and articulate in our own language. You can discern this purpose by asking yourself discovery questions at different times and in different ways, always noting your answers until you can say, "Aha, this feels like my core purpose." Such discovery questions are simple: What is my purpose? What is my mission in life? What am I here to accomplish? How do I want to be remembered?

Sometimes, our purpose just shows up and we know it's true. Often, we are living our purpose, yet have not owned and articulated it in a mindful way. But discovering purpose can require effort. For some, it may involve asking God for assistance, and then contemplating the questions. Or, it might take creating a special time for reflection and then responding to the questions in writing. Initially, your answer may be a lengthy statement. This is a significant beginning, yet over time it is wise to focus your purpose into a short phrase or statement that you can readily access for inspiration or focus.

In my indigenous culture, purpose is so significant that we have several tools to assist people in its discovery, including the journey, vision quest, sweat lodge, and guided ceremony. When my nephew Canek was in his teen years, his mother took him for a month-long camping journey through the Yucatan area of Mexico, in part so he could discover his indigenous roots.[3] A year later, my brother took him to the local hills to fast and pray, while family and friends prayed in the sweat lodge that he would find inspiration and direction. Each of these experiences contributed to Canek's connection to self and environment, his developing world view, and evolving his purpose.

Over the years, I have developed several ceremonies to help people discover, reconnect with, or evolve their purpose. Activists are often involved in intense and prolonged work that weighs on us physically and emotionally. We need to reconnect with our purpose to determine how it has evolved or changed and to restore our energy. Here, the ceremony usually involves creating sacred time and guiding the person in meditation to visit those places and experiences that can assist him or her in connecting to purpose. The intent is to open the person to intuition or spirit and invite helpful messages to surface. If you feel such a need, consider visiting my Web site at www.robertovargas.com to access a guided meditation exercise called "Reconnecting with Purpose."

Mature activists recognize that living one's purpose is not a singular event, but a lifelong practice. We discover our purpose, use it to guide our lives, reconnect and evaluate it, and then deepen or evolve its meaning. Connecting with purpose is a practice that inspires and brings focus to our lives, and prepares us for leadership. Because we are committed to the development of others, we pay attention for the opportunity to assist family and friends in discovering and living their purpose as well.

Your Personal Success Path

We want success for our family and friends. Here, the idea of success is not necessarily material abundance and leisure living, but what success truly means for you. For me, success is living a good life in which you are taking care of yourself and those you love. It is living your purpose, making progress toward personal and family goals, bettering the world, and enjoying life.

Getting your act together involves creating your own success plan and moving forward on your path. You are continually learning to access your power, achieve goals, and learn from your experience. When you are living this type of success, you are in a better position to be a teacher and supporter of growth for family and friends.

Success begins with forming a positive attitude and recognizing your power. Often, reminding ourselves of our brilliance and positive intentions can help. You might start your day by telling yourself something like: *Life is fantastic! I am a great person who deserves joy and happiness. I have the intelligence and abilities to achieve my goals. Together with others I can make the world better.*

We can also enhance our attitude by acknowledging our blessings. Gratitude lifts attitude. For years I used a ritual to boost my attitude that became even more effective when I incorporated some of the teachings of Anthony Robbins, a world-renowned success coach and trainer.[4] This approach begins with taking a power walk. It can be around your house or wherever you go for inspiration. Walk with an exaggerated self-confident and joyful attitude, saying aloud what you are grateful for. You might start with your life and health, and continue to include your family, friends, job, and so forth.

Once you start feeling your energy lift, shift your statements to express confidence in yourself. Begin with stating and repeating with power, "I have all that I need to achieve what I want." Hear what you are saying, and mean it. Then get more particular with your exclamations, "I have all the commitment I need to be a great daughter!" "I have all the love I need to be a great teacher!" "I have all the experience I need to make this project succeed!" Do this for at least ten minutes a day for thirteen days, and your attitude will become more positive and confident. Then do as I do, incorporate a little boosting every morning or whenever it is needed during the day.

Success requires clarity of purpose, and also goals and action plans. Let's say that as an activist, your purpose is to become a better person and to stop the incarceration of youth. Once you are clear on your purpose, then clarify your goals and action plans. What is my personal development goal for this year? What two or three objectives can I commit to for making the changes I desire for our youth? What is my action plan, the specific actions I will take to advance these goals?

If you haven't formulated your key goals or if you believe your action plans could use a tune-up, I strongly suggest that you take about ten minutes to engage in the following goal clarification exercise. Even if you are clear on your goals, doing this exercise will provide familiarity with an important tool you can use to help family and friends develop their goals and action plans.

Developing My Action Plan

First, pull out a notebook page and write down everything you would like to accomplish or be in your life. Write until you reach the bottom of the page. Review your list and then choose the most important three to five items. Now state each of your hopes as a goal. Using the general format indicated below, develop your goal sheet. First state one of your goals, then list why it is important to accomplish or the benefits that will come from its achievement. Then identify the action steps required to implement each goal, including projected due dates. Finally, list a couple of people to share your goals with who will help you stay on track, and what affirmation you will use to keep your energy positive and directed toward your success. Affirmations are positive statements that validate your talents and power, such as "I have all the intelligence and heart I need to inspire others to participate."

My Goal: *Develop a side business for green landscaping and home gardening*

Why Important (the benefits to you or others):
- *Helps others develop yards that produce food, conserve water, and prevent waste*
- *Creates balance in my life—political activism and working with life*
- *Generates income doing something I love*
- *Encourages me to continue learning about what interests me*

Action Steps and Due Dates
1. *Identify requirements to begin business: October 30*
2. *Determine how landscaper consultants charge for services: November 15*
3. *Identify courses I should take, e.g., using computer for landscape plans, specific courses on "green" landscaping: November 15*
4. *Develop business plan: January 30*
5. *Start business (at least 1–2 clients): March 15*

People I will tell who can support me:
- *Brother David—he'll keep me on task and provide support*
- *Cousin Sylvia—her enthusiasm about gardening will keep me motivated*
- *Friend Eric—he has business knowledge and many contacts*

My Affirmation: *I have all the discipline and enthusiasm I need to be successful! My business will make the world better!*

Success is then enjoyed in the doing. Keep your goals in mind, build your energy, cultivate supportive relationships, practice communication, use financial sense, and evolve your spiritual connection. These are the best practices for achieving goals and living success. Some of these practices become goals in themselves, as we dedicate time to maintain good health and vibrant energy, or to build supportive relationships. Remember that living success involves balance and taking time to enjoy life as we pursue our multiple goals.

Getting your act together does not mean waiting until you are perfect to engage in being a teacher or role model for family and friends. Our role as family activists is to both embrace our positive nature and pursue our success, while we also help others recognize their inherent goodness and realize their potential. This way, together we create the good life we desire for all people.

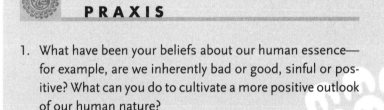

PRAXIS

1. What have been your beliefs about our human essence— for example, are we inherently bad or good, sinful or positive? What can you do to cultivate a more positive outlook of our human nature?

2. In one sentence or phrase, how would you state your purpose? Does reading your statement inspire you? If so, consider writing it down and placing it where you can periodically see it. If it doesn't enthuse you, consider rewriting it until you feel the statement reflects who you are and your commitments. Remember that your statement can change and evolve—this is not necessarily your statement for always.

3. Regarding your personal success or development path, what needs attention? Which goal will you prioritize for this next period, and what are your next three action steps?

6

CREATING FAMILY CONNECTIONS

● ●

Our goal is to develop such connection among family and friends that they see themselves as sharing a "common unity" where supporting each other is desired and comes easily. The most powerful means to foster this connection is by doing *conocimiento* (sharing conversation to know each other) and applying the Unity Principle. Doing *conocimiento* is the essential tool we can use to connect people, and the Unity Principle is a formula to help us realize the many opportunities we encounter every day to increase group harmony and power. The intent of this chapter is to deepen your understanding of *conocimiento* and the Unity Principle toward enhancing your ability to increase family interconnection, unity, and power, and create beloved community.

Conocimiento Is Creating Connection

Think about the times when you and family members are working in close relationship. You coordinate schedules to help each other or share conversations to encourage each other's growth. In these instances the support flows because there is a feeling of connection.

Where does this connection come from? Is it inherent in your blood relationship, does it come from years of experience together, or is it an unspoken commitment you made to each other years back? All these set the foundation and contribute to your relationship, yet the real connection occurs when you take time to meaningfully get to know each other. Among Chicanos we call this process doing *conocimiento*, actively sharing about ourselves to create connection.

If you look up *conocimiento* in a Spanish dictionary, it has multiple meanings as a noun—it is knowledge, understanding, and acquaintance. The verb *conocer* means to know, meet, become acquainted with, or to know another or self. In its popular form, *conocimiento* means "to nurture connection by sharing knowledge of each other."

I am doing *conocimiento* when I meet a new person, extend my hand, share who I am, and ask several questions to invite him or her to similarly share. This is doing *conocimiento* to know another. I am also doing *conocimiento* when I sit down with my mother or daughter and ask, "What's going on in your life?" This is doing *conocimiento* to nurture and deepen our connection. It is never enough to be related; we have to engage in communication that keeps us connected.

Conocimiento is an essential skill and strategy not only for family activists, but for all people who desire healthier families, work groups, and organizations. Yet, focusing upon our families, we know that for members to enjoy being family, share support, and even participate in community service, we need to continually foster our connection. We need to be sharing conversation, asking or responding to questions that help us know each other in meaningful ways. Informally or more formally, we need to share on such themes as: What are you experiencing? What challenges are you facing? What brings you joy? Sharing with each other about such questions keeps us informed in a way that maintains or deepens our connection, and nurtures love and power.

Love is nurtured because our continual sharing creates more connection. Every one of the experiences, feelings, or ideas we share creates more connection as we expand our understanding of each other. Additionally, sharing provides us information that invites new opportunities for extending support. Knowing my friend is going through difficult times, and knowing her tendency to become glued to her computer work, I can find ways to encourage her to take breaks or send inspirational quotes to lift her spirits. Doing *conocimiento* with her over time has enabled me to know her in a way in which I am better able to support her.

Similarly, power is fostered. Power means possessing the ability to make things happen. We have more power in our relationships when we are connected. Whether it is to clean the garage, organize a family gathering, or mobilize friends to participate in a demonstration, we have more power to accomplish any task to the degree that we know and trust each other and share connection. The deeper we develop mutual understanding and connection, the greater the power we have. This is the basis of the Unity Principle, which I describe below.

In my work as a planning consultant, organizations and companies hire me to facilitate *conocimiento*, not so much to foster love, but to do team building. Essentially, I assist team members to get to know each other more deeply so they can work together more effectively and creatively. This is another form of applying *conocimiento* to optimize group unity and power.

The Unity Principle

The Unity Principle calls upon activists or organizers to involve groups in developing relationships of connection and trust that can lead to increased unity and power. I discovered the Unity Principle when I was director of a newly formed counseling center. My responsibility included organizing teams of staff, volunteers, and community members to work on a variety of projects. We had committees and work groups to advocate for funding, develop services for youth, recruit volunteers, support parents in developing an alternative school, and encourage community participation in local issues.

Working with these various groups I observed differences in the quality of the group experience. In several groups, ideas flowed, members readily volunteered, and people appeared to enjoy working with each other. In other groups, members appeared committed to the task, but the energy, enthusiasm, and creativity were not as strong. I noticed that the more vibrant groups possessed a community feeling as people were doing *conocimiento* as part of their work. They enjoyed working together because they were actively connecting.

Doing conocimiento *strengthens connection and develops unity.*

Given these observations, I incorporated time for sharing within the meetings I facilitated. After presenting the agenda, I would ask participants to briefly share on several questions to strengthen our connection. Of new groups, I would ask questions like: Where are you from? What should we know about you to help us in our work? With other groups, I would request a brief check-in—How are you doing today?—or ask about expectations for the meeting. Typically, these brief sharings were enough to connect the members of the group, enhance rapport, and create a working environment for fun and accomplishment.

Over time, more of us applied the Unity Principle to our group work, having participants do *conocimiento* to develop connection, unity, and power. We would invite participants to get to know each other by having them share where they were from and why attending this meeting was important to them. Group members would immediately discover commonalities or interesting differences and feel more connected. Later we continued with check-ins at each meeting, using strategic questions to deepen the connection or to prepare the group for its immediate work. We learned that the most effective *conocimiento* questions were easy to understand, provided substantive or interesting information, and could be answered in a minute or two. If more time was available, we could extend the time and allow for deeper sharing.

Essentially, the Unity Principle reminds us to find ways to facilitate and encourage sharing among family or team members to increase the group's connection, unity, and ability to accomplish tasks together. As illustrated by the diagram below, we encourage or do *conocimiento* to make connection easy. The more connections we form with another person, we create a quality and spirit of unity which provides the basis for increased power—the ability for the relationship or group to act on common concerns.

Enthused with this principle, my colleagues and I sought its application in other types of group situations, particularly in community meetings with dozens of people present, and then later within families. The idea of applying the principle to families came at the time I described in Chapter 4, when I turned to my family for inspirational support to find that our unity, so vibrant before, was disrupted. Although there were several causes of the conflicts in my family, a chief reason was that we had lost connection with each other. We had not maintained active *conocimiento*, and the only way we were going to heal our wounds and restore our connection was to commit to

Unity Principle

Conocimiento

Connection

Unity

Power

reknowing each other. This idea guided me in all that I did to organize and facilitate our first family council.

I had engaged each family member in a one-to-one *conocimiento* to establish a reconnection that I thought would bring them to participate in our family gathering. The exercise I started with—that we each share our best qualities—deepened our understanding of each other. When the idea arose at our family meeting to have us all identify the positive qualities of each other, I asked that we include the qualities of our absent brothers, knowing that this *conocimiento* would help us to more fully see them, and would also provide me a powerful way to extend the *conocimiento* process by later sharing the information with them. All this *conocimiento* was to develop the connection and unity that could enable us to address the conflicts injuring our family. Building off our reconnection, we came to incorporate doing *conocimiento* on an ongoing basis to keep our connection vibrant and to continue learning about and from each other. Subsequent sharing taught us more about how we could be allies not only to our brother Jack, but to all gay and lesbian people.

The application of *conocimiento* to family should have been common sense, yet at the time the idea of applying the Unity Principle in this way was a major "aha." Just as work or community groups need opportunities to get to know each other, families need to nurture and maintain their connection. Just because we grew up with family doesn't mean we came to know each other fully, or that our connection will automatically continue, even when we live in the same house. We must invest energy to engage in *conocimiento*. We do it by creating time for the one-to-one and group conversations that inform us, our family and friends, about each other's lives and thoughts.

Doing *Conocimiento*

Whether your commitment is to increase the well-being of family, community, or society, you need skills to facilitate people connecting with each other. By incorporating *conocimiento* as an ongoing practice, you can enrich your life and to do the same for others.

Start your practice by initiating and guiding meaningful one-to-one conversations. This way you learn skills and strategies that will help you facilitate connecting people in all situations, from informal conversations to large group gatherings.

When doing one-to-one *conocimiento*, start by clarifying your reason for having the conversation. Knowing your purpose enables you to be more authentic and strategic in your interaction. Generally, we do *conocimiento* to discover, understand, and connect with another. If the person is a nephew or niece, maybe your purpose is to develop a relationship to enable subsequent teaching or collaboration. With your parents, your intent might be to experience a warmer connection with each other.

For doing *conocimiento*, keep these four guiding points in mind: (1) good introduction, (2) great questions, (3) active listening, and (4) balanced sharing.

Good Introduction

In our society, distractions—from television to video games—are so pervasive that many people fail to learn or are forgetting how to share meaningful conversation. For this reason, it is important to initiate *conocimiento* in a way that engages the involvement of the other person.

Given my father's personality, I would usually contact him ahead of time to let him know of my intention. "Dad, I'm coming by the house. Can we schedule time to catch up? I want to hear what's going on with you. Also, I might need some counsel from you." Inviting him to speak was usually enough to interest him, but expressing my potential need for counsel would ensure his commitment.

Connecting with my daughters is different. Our relationships have evolved so that I can approach either of them and simply ask, how about getting together for some *conocimiento*? We know what that means and we make it happen. It wasn't always that easy, particularly during their teen years. With Cheli, my approach often sounded like this: "I have a favor to ask. I'd love for us to catch up with each other. Can we share some *conocimiento* time? You can choose when." If we were going to share time, she had to feel the power of making the choice. Now, either can simply call and say, "What's up?" which means, let's do some *conocimiento*.

Great Questions

Once the commitment is secured, think about questions or themes that will be meaningful to both of you. With my brothers or friends, it is usually sharing: "Tell me what's going great, and also what are the challenges?" This question always helps us get current with each other. In addition, it provides each of us the opportunity for thera-peutic release of frustrations or worries. Being able to "download" about our difficulties then enables us to enjoy talking about the good that we are contributing to the world. Visiting my aunt, I will tell her in Spanish that I've stopped by to hear about the family and about something "positive" happening. I find this benefits us both because it adds to our inspiration.

Active Listening

In doing *conocimiento* our objective is to *hear* the other person and nurture our connection. This requires active listening. This is not lis-tening while thinking about your response, or continually chiming in with a "me too" story, but deeply listening to understand and per-mit connection. A repeated criticism I would hear from my young daughters about adults was that they may sometimes ask good questions, but they don't listen. Active listening means being fully present and asking questions to enable us to fully understand the other person's story or thoughts.

Balanced Sharing

Some people find sharing about themselves threatening or difficult. For this reason, it is often helpful, once you and the other person have agreed on the *conocimiento* plan, to begin by sharing first. "I'd like us to hear about how our lives are going, and I'm happy to go first. Is that okay?" This provides you the opportunity to model the process of sharing, and also to demonstrate that you are not just ask-ing them to disclose but are willing to share yourself. This is espe-cially relevant when you are just starting doing *conocimiento* with others.

Facilitating Group Connection

How often have you been in a gathering of family and friends where, though there was lots of talking, at the end of the evening you didn't feel that you actually connected with anyone or shared in meaningful conversation? For deeper contact, sometimes there is the need for someone to informally serve as a facilitator. With sensitive facilitation and support almost any family gathering can be made inspirational and nurture group *conocimiento*. Whether it is an informal dinner conversation or a birthday party involving dozens of people, the opportunity exists to facilitate meaningful family connection. The following discussion assumes that you are serving your group as a facilitator dedicated to encouraging *conocimiento*.

For most families, the informal approach to doing *conocimiento* works best. While the family is sitting around the dinner table, you can present your request: "I would love to hear some family stories. Could we all take turns and share one of our best family experiences?" You might encounter resistance as someone says it will take too long, or "I can't think of anything to share." So you offer, "How about we each take about three or four minutes, and I'll start so you have time to recall your story."

For families not accustomed to such sharing, this request may be too significant of a change to manage alone. Some preparatory work may be required. You may need to identify an ally—such as a supportive sister, parent, or friend—prior to the gathering, explain your intent, and request support. Explain that your vision is greater family connection and your plan is to begin the practice of sharing with each other. You might ask your ally to support your proposal at the dinner table and be ready to volunteer if necessary. The power of two or more collaborating to introduce *conocimiento* rarely fails.

If you have a degree of authority and respect in your family, you can be more direct in announcing your vision and the plan. "I love our family and feel we can be more connected and supportive of each other. I'd like us to strengthen our connection by doing some personal sharing as a group. Can we commit to an evening to share a conversation that can help us better know each other? Can we use next Friday's dinner to share about what is going on in our lives and any hopes or plans we have for this coming year?"

Once your family has agreed with your proposal, you have a family *conocimiento* session to convene and facilitate. Convening involves actually getting the group together, and facilitation is guiding the conversation.

Before the chosen date, remind the family of the meeting. At dinner you announce when it's time to begin the conversation. To start the meeting, remind the group that a healthy family actively connects, and that the purpose of the evening is to provide everyone the opportunity to catch up with each other. Also remind them that you will be facilitating the meeting, which means that you will keep the group on track and ensure that everyone gets their turn to speak. Depending on the family culture, you may or may not want to offer guidelines. For some families it's helpful to be explicit. "I'd like us to commit to listening to each other with minimal interruptions. Let's say we each have about four minutes to share. I will let you know when you have a couple of minutes left. I hope we will all share, yet anyone is free to pass. Who would like to start?"

Ideally, everyone shares with minimal intervention required by you. Yet, with most families, jokes and tangential issues will surface, along with bona fide questions. As the facilitator, your role is to coordinate the dialogue traffic. You might have to remind the group that someone is still speaking, determine whether to allow questions, or request to deal with questions after everyone shares. When the group finishes, you then facilitate a closing, which ideally includes three elements—reflections on the sharing, exploration for follow-up, and final feeling words.

Reflect on the Sharing

In introducing *conocimiento*, we are encouraging a family culture where dialogue, learning, and collaboration become the norm. So, ideally, the first *conocimiento* cultivates the idea of ongoing sharing and connection. For this reason, when the group completes sharing, you engage participants in a "reflection moment" and ask for their thoughts about the *conocimiento*. What did the family members think or feel about the sharing? The vast majority of the time, family and friends affirm the value of the experience. They usually say things like it was great to share, we needed more time, it was amazing how much we didn't know about each other, and it was inspiring. You then use their expressions to negotiate a commitment to follow up.

Follow-up

This is when you pose the question, can we do this again? If so, decide when, and ask what questions or themes the group wants to address in future meetings. Also ask if there are any suggestions for the next meeting. Given our activist orientation, we could suggest that at a future gathering we ask each other how it is that we are living love and fairness or creating good in the world. These types of questions are powerful because they offer participants a lens through which to consider their actions during the coming period, and then the opportunity for everyone to experience validation as they subsequently share and learn from each other's diverse deeds. Ideally, we can encourage the group to commit to one or more subsequent family sharing sessions, and then to commit to a practice of periodic *conocimiento* that fits the family culture. For some families, it becomes part of an informal practice that may occur every month or at special holidays, a dinner gathering, or an outing at the park. For those families who can only gather every year or so, it becomes part of their reunion experience.

For future occasions, if the family commits to a longer time for *conocimiento*, the facilitator may propose several rounds of sharing. Each round provides everyone the opportunity to address a specific question, and then each person is invited to respond to the next question. With this approach, the first round is usually a warm-up where the family is asked to respond to something like, "How was your day?" The second round is for deeper questions like, "Ideally, what are three things you would like to accomplish this coming year?" A final round could be to express appreciation for someone else in the family.

To coordinate turns to speak, the facilitator may ask participants to simply volunteer as they desire or ask the group to begin with the first volunteer and continue clockwise around the circle. For some families, it helps to introduce the use of the talking stick or a similar tool, which will be elaborated upon in Chapter 10.

Closing Words

Finally, to close the conversation or gathering, ask if each person can offer a word or phrase to describe their current feeling. Often positive sentiments are offered—"more united," "inspired," "proud," "hopeful," "connected." With this expression, the family validates for itself the power of the experience and develops their ability to share thoughts and feelings. If other feeling words come up like "sad," "disappointed," "frustrated," and so on, the group may want to explore what is going on for this person, or it may be left as your homework to pursue individually. Thank the group for their participation and immediately check in with those who expressed the difficult feelings. Let each know you are concerned about the feeling they shared, and ask if they would like to talk further. Whatever they share will extend the communication and provide important learning for both of you.

Challenges Doing *Conocimiento*

As you have been reading, you may have been considering how you might serve your family as a facilitator. If so, you may be wondering, is every *conocimiento* conversation a success? Or, what happens if a messy issue comes up? I would say that most *conocimiento* gatherings represent a success because the experience is often a first step for a family to improve their communication and connection. Yet in the moment it may not feel like a success because difficult issues do surface.

By doing *conocimiento* we often create the opportunity for families to communicate unexpressed feelings and concerns. Because the environment feels safe, family members sometimes expose unexpected issues. A son may say, "I can't do this because I'm angry at Dad," or a daughter may say, "This is stupid because we never listen to each other." Here, if you are the parent or another person with authority within the family, then of course you need to respond in a responsible way. Similarly, if you have assumed or been granted the authority of the facilitator, you have a responsibility to point the group toward a positive resolution. So, in both situations, you must validate the concern and then help the family identify an appropriate way and time to address the issue.

For example, to the angry son the facilitator might respond: "I hear your anger. Part of the reason for this sharing is to get to the place where we can be more honest and supportive of each other. I ask that we continue with our group sharing, and when we finish I'll commit to sitting with you and Dad to hear your concerns." It is important that you validate the concern, ask support to keep the group on course, and offer a resolution strategy.

Similarly, for the daughter, you validate her concern, speak to "our intent to improve communication in the family," and offer a resolution: "Just like you, I have concerns about the family—I believe we all do. So after our sharing can we as a group develop a list of improvements we want to see in the family, and then schedule another meeting to work on them?" Or, better yet, ask the group for help: "One of us has presented an issue that needs attention. Can we finish our sharing and then consider ideas to resolve this concern?"

Regarding the unexpected messy issues that may surface, the best principles to follow are to fully try to listen to and appreciate the concern being raised, respond in a genuine way that recognizes the person speaking, and enlist the larger group to help find a win-win resolution that can ultimately lead to increased unity and understanding.

Creative Group *Conocimiento* for Unity, Inspiration, and Vision

After our kids attend a family or social function, I'll often ask them, "How was it?" Invariably, their reflections include the quality of *conocimiento*, and whether the event inspired them or not. Either the event was great and inspiring because people were connecting, or it was sad because it was hard to connect with others and there was no uplifting sharing. Once you experience the power of *conocimiento* for connecting family, you will see how its inclusion within any gathering can not only foster increased unity, but also inspire pride, vision, and commitment. We develop a higher standard for what constitutes a great gathering—people connected! As family activists, we begin doing *conocimiento* in one-to-one and small group conversations, and develop our skills to facilitate creative *conocimiento* on behalf of larger family or community gatherings, as illustrated in the following examples.

To Build Family Unity

We were honored to be among the fifty people attending my wife's niece's pre-wedding family potluck in Topeka, Kansas. As most of Valerie Mendoza and George Hartley's respective families and close friends lived in separate states and did not know each other, the intent of this gathering was to nurture connection among everyone attending, and I was asked to facilitate. Before the dinner began, I welcomed everyone on behalf of the wedding couple, explained our intention, and then initiated our "connecting plan." Everyone first introduced themselves, sharing where they were from and their relationship to the couple. Then, during dinner, everyone was asked to meet at least two people they didn't know and share with them what they liked best about either Valerie or George.

After dinner, I facilitated some group reflection and then our closing words. I encouraged everyone to gather in a circle, and invited reflections from the group to help them more deeply experience and value their recent exchanges. First I asked people how it felt to meet and share with a "new family member." All the brief comments were positive, echoing the first statement made: "It feels like I am really expanding my family." Next, we shared what we had learned about the couple. You could feel the pride felt by every family member as they heard the positive qualities of the bride and groom being recognized and celebrated. We ended with everyone in the circle holding hands and expressing a final feeling word. The tone we set that evening continued throughout the wedding festivities over the next couple of days. Relationships were developed between the two families, and everyone felt inspired that families of two different cultures, Mexican-American and Irish-American, could come together and quickly grow to feel genuine connection with each other.

To Inspire Community Commitment

In their Chicago community, the Gonzales family is credited with initiating numerous community service agencies and programs. For years, Lupe Reyes and her daughter, Mary Gonzales, were the moving force for the family, modeling and encouraging a caring spirit and community action by all family and friends. Committed to keeping this activist tradition strong a generation later, Grandmother Lupe initiated the practice of doing an annual *conocimiento* regarding the family's involvement in community service as part of their annual Christmas gathering.

Typically, most of Grandmother Lupe's eleven adult children attend the gathering along with their children and grandchildren. Congregating in the adjoining living and dining rooms, the children sit in a middle circle close to the grandmother while the adults gather around. In a discussion facilitated by one of the aunts, the families are first asked to announce significant family developments or special reasons for gratitude. Then the children and youth are asked by Grandmother Lupe, "What are you doing this year to serve others?" Young and old speak, sometimes sharing about their projects and other times requesting the greater family to support their particular community service. Afterward there is an exchange of gifts, usually between godparents and their children.

Twenty-five-year-old granddaughter Donna feels tremendous pride and inspiration from these gatherings, which reflect her family's strong community service tradition. "Community involvement is our family tradition, but knowing that Grandmother is going to be asking makes you think about it throughout the year. Then during this evening we get to hear all the incredible things our family is doing. It's inspiring!" Donna sees the commitment lived by her grandmother and parents continuing in her own life as an attorney, a family member, and someday as a mother.

To Inspire Vision

When good friends Eduardo García and Rosa María Rivera organize a birthday party for their children, they include all their family and friends, and the adults often outnumber the children. A description of one of their early parties illustrates how the gatherings are used to inspire vision and foster beloved community.

Upon my arrival, Rosa recruits me to facilitate a *conocimiento* circle before the birthday cake. Using a large spoon and a pot lid, we call the picnic crowd together. After brief welcoming words, I announce that we are here to celebrate Eddie and Diego's birthdays, and before we bring out the cake we want the young people present to hear from all of us about "the world we want for these kids," and why we are here. In response to the first question, participants chime in their vision with words like "peace," "a healthy Earth," "no war," "education for all," "much love," and "loving *familia*."

To transition to the second question, I ask the group to recall the vision we have just articulated for our children and ask that, in the spirit of this hope, we briefly introduce who we are and why we are here. The unruly noise level drops and people introduce themselves. The feeling of inspiration rises as we hear each other share. Articulated in various ways, the group expresses that we are present to feel the connection of *familia* and community, and to reinspire ourselves and each other to continue working for a better world for our kids.

Fifteen years after the party described above, Eduardo and Rosa María continue to organize such parties for their kids, yet now the number of young people has increased as they invite all their friends to experience the "unity circle." Over the years of doing *conocimiento*, acquaintances have become family to each other, and many have become collaborators in numerous projects serving the community, from supporting the schools and projects of each other's children to organizing peace demonstrations. Now many look forward to the unity circle that is part of every family/community gathering, because it reaffirms the family connection and reinspires their commitment to live good lives.

As family activists, one of our intentions is to continually seek or develop opportunities to facilitate increased connection and unity among family and friends. As we practice doing *conocimiento* we become ever more confident and creative in applying it within all our family and community gatherings.

PRAXIS

1. *Conocimiento* represents a powerful idea. How would you explain its meaning to your family or friends?

2. How current are you with some of your closest family and friends? With whom do you need to commit time to catch up and reconnect? Schedule a time to sit together and do the connecting. Afterward note what you learned from your experience about doing *conocimiento*.

3. What benefits can you see in doing *conocimiento* within your family, organization, or group? Begin considering how you might initiate or facilitate doing *conocimiento*. When could you do it? Whom could you enlist to serve as an ally? You may find the specific tools for facilitating group sharing presented in Chapter 10 helpful in initiating your *conocimiento* plan.

7
CO-POWERING TO
BATTLE EL NO

⬤ ⬤

A remarkable statement from Marianne Williamson begins, "Our deepest fear is not that we are inadequate. Our deepest fear is that we are powerful beyond measure."[1] While inadequacy may not be our deepest fear, it is often a deep wound, and the truth is that too many of us carry feelings of inadequacy that limit us. To advance a healthier society we must understand what undermines our power and how we become empowered. Toward this end, this chapter elaborates on the concept of *EL NO*, the negativity that limits our power, and co-powering, the process of empowering others and our relationships.

The Great Turning, the shifting of our world to the positive, requires all caring people to accept and develop their power to make good happen for themselves, their families, and our society. Key to this goal is developing our skills to empower each other. We can do this by engaging in co-powering communication, and consciously confronting the negativity that undermines our personal, family, and community power.

There are multiple reasons why we are not advancing the positive change we desire in the world. One central reason is that as individuals, families, or communities we are not fully owning and developing our power. Many of us have been socialized or brainwashed to accept an image of ourselves that limits our ability to fully tap our knowledge, talents, and energy to achieve what is important to us. A vast majority of our society struggles with varying degrees of a nagging self-doubt that says, I am not good, smart, or worthy enough to achieve my personal goals, let alone the larger goals for community change. Therefore, a critical task of all activists is to be the friend and coach who aids family, friends, and others to love themselves and accept their power.

Every day we have numerous occasions to interact with family, friends, or associates. Whether it is extending a "good morning," a casual conversation, or a significant communication, we have the choice of making it ordinary or inspiring. For me, quality communication occurs when we consciously choose to lift the confidence of the other, as well as of oneself. Co-powering occurs when our actions develop the power of the other, our relationship, and ourselves, toward advancing a greater good for all.

Our society bombards us with such negativity that large numbers of people struggle with depression and powerlessness. They feel they are not worthy to be loved or intelligent enough to succeed. We can turn this around and nurture a culture of self-confidence and a "can do" attitude by actively engaging in co-powering. We start with families and friends, and continue with our co-workers and neighbors. Ultimately, the Great Turning requires a movement in which everyone actively participates in raising each other's personal and collective power.

Our Worst Enemy: *EL NO*

It is amazing how a simple idea can have a tremendous impact on the way we view ourselves and upon our ability to reclaim our power. This is the case with *EL NO*, a concept we invented within the Latino community to explain the dynamics of disempowerment we experienced as working class, nonwhite people. Yet, understanding its dynamics among Latinos provides invaluable insights for all caring people into why *all of us* are not fully utilizing our power, and what needs to be done to liberate each other and our greater society from the negativity that undermines our personal and community power. Because I believe that understanding *EL NO* is fundamental to effective family activism, I ask that you apply both your mind and heart to the following discussion. I believe it will make you a far more sensitive person and effective activist.

Have you ever experienced a feeling of self-doubt or panic coupled with an internal voice screaming, "You can't do it"? This is the voice of *EL NO*. Within our minds, we all have a voice that affirms our power, saying, "Hey, you can do it!" and another that negates our power, usually loudly saying, "You're too dumb and stupid, so forget even trying." When we established *El Centro de Salud Mental* (the Mental Health Center) in 1973, its explicit mission was to empower Latino individuals and families. The following presents what we learned about the disempowering process of *EL NO* and consequently the process of empowerment. Because we worked on this issue in Spanish, I use key Spanish words to explain how we came to unravel this phenomenon that actually affects all people.

During the early years of *El Centro de Salud Mental*, our staff dedicated a meeting each month to dialogue about strategies for people empowerment. At one such meeting, Francisco M. Hernandez shared about the challenges he was encountering in recruiting Chicano youth to learn the skill of silk-screening.[2] His objective was to build self-esteem by providing youth a means for self-expression by designing messages for posters or T-shirts. However, as he approached young people, he continually heard the same response, "*No puedo*" (I can't do it). Immediately several of our counselors responded that his experience resonated with what they were hearing from clients when challenged to create change for themselves: "*No puedo*." With hesitancy, many of us recalled experiencing that horrifying feeling of self-doubt ourselves, when we too had either felt or said, *no puedo*. Aided with this insight, we then proceeded to explore the origins of the feeling behind the words *no puedo*, which figuratively means "I have no power."

Here I am going to use my childhood experience to illustrate the origins of what we began to call *EL NO*, both the internal voice that denies our power and a disempowering concept of self. Child psychologists inform us that children develop their essential understanding about themselves and life by the time they are five to seven years old. Now, using myself as an example, I will explain how many children of color grow up denying their power and are drawn into a dynamic of internalized oppression.

All the professional people I encountered as a young child—
chiefly doctors, teachers, and other people of authority—were members of the dominant white culture. Unconsciously this led me to
believe that only white people were successful. The message that I
internalized was *no pueden*, or, "You brown people can't." During
my first days of school, my name, Roberto, was changed to Bobbie,
and Spanish became a forbidden language. The core message I was
receiving was *no vales* (you have no value)—your language, culture,
and people are not worthy of respect. This message of *no vales* continued during those early years, when nothing in my school experience validated anything positive about my culture. Like every other
child, I also received my daily dose of television images, devoid of
anyone who looked like me except for the occasional Latino janitor
or gang members. Again, seeing only images of white people suc-
ceeding, the message I received was, "You people are not good or
capable enough." Before I turned eight years old, a relatively self-
confident child had been assaulted by so many messages of invali-
dation that the internal messenger that said "No, you can't" became
considerably louder and stronger. I had unconsciously adopted the
attitude of *no puedo*. Part of my mind had been coerced to deny my
value.

As a result, for many years I became my own worst enemy, as I
would deny my ability to engage in new or challenging activities.
That internalized voice would repeatedly undermine my inquisi-
tiveness by yanking me back, saying, "Hey, you can't succeed at
that, you're not smart or white enough." Fortunately, I had also
received strong validating messages from family, particularly my
grandmother, that boosted my self-esteem and cultivated a voice of
self-affirmation. Like many in my community, I consequently grew
up with two voices in my head, one saying, "You're bright, you can
do it!" and the other declaring, "Who are you to think you can?" Are
you familiar with these two voices? As a child, did you experience
messages that invalidated your self-esteem and power? Because of
the nurturing quality of the family affirmations I received, in time
the positive voice became stronger than the voice of *EL NO*. Yet,
many other Latinos were not so fortunate; the messages of *EL NO*
were so pervasive and the validations so rare that *EL NO* became

more than just a strong negating voice. It became a chronic mind-set that thwarts their positive potential.

The greater tragedy is that this not only happens to Latinos, but to blacks, Asians, women, gays, lesbians, and even white males. All children today are subjected to a steady stream of messages flowing from family, church, school, and media that undermine our power. These messages are continually reminding us that we are not good, smart, or attractive enough to be successful (that is, unless you purchase a certain advertised product). Additionally, depending on our culture or gender, we must contend with powerful disempowering stereotypes perpetuated by our society: Minorities are not intelligent, women are too emotional, gays are not normal, men can't change. Consequently, for many people the negative assaults upon their psyches are so persistent, while uplifting messages are so infrequent, that *EL NO* becomes the prominent voice within their minds. These people become handicapped in their pursuit of personal success, and our society loses precious energy and creativity that could potentially be applied to bettering our world.

Despite loving their children, many parents do not know how to foster their self-esteem. We tend to criticize rather than praise. From our church and religion we often receive the message that we are inherently sinful rather than possessing divine potential. Most of our schools deny our intelligence by treating us as empty receptacles only capable of receiving information.

These influences of *EL NO* are not only debilitating to individuals, we must also contend with the patterns of negativity that further undermine our self-esteem among each other and our communities. Many who struggle with *EL NO* tend to invalidate not only self, but also those around them. The dynamic is unconscious, yet one who has been socialized to believe oneself is unworthy often demeans others to lift their own self-esteem. We criticize others to feel better about ourselves. We make comments like, "Why are you applying to college, you know you're not smart enough," or "I don't know why John is being promoted; he really isn't that competent." Our unconscious practice becomes putting others down to lift ourselves up.

While our initial tendency may be to demean those closest to us, too often we move to project our negativity upon other people, and then upon our entire society. We make comments like, "You can't trust Jews, they're just for themselves." "Forget the youth, they are totally apathetic." "Men are insensitive." "You can't trust politicians." "People are too apathetic to create change." "Humans are inherently selfish." The result is that we become a society so steeped in negativity that we refuse to believe in our human potential and ability to advance positive change—the negation of our personal power becomes a negation of our community and social power.

EL NO must be halted. We must all become part of the force that transforms *EL NO*. We can do this by choosing to accept our goodness and power, and becoming people who continually seek to validate and affirm the positive potential of others. Again, words from Marianne Williamson can provide us with inspiration and guidance: "We were born to manifest the glory of God that is within us. It's not just in some of us; it's in everyone. And as we let our light shine, we unconsciously give other people permission to do the same. As we are liberated from our own fear, our presence automatically liberates others."[3] Our task is to liberate ourselves and others from *EL NO*, and inspire an attitude of positive possibility.

Transform EL NO

Understanding the dynamic of *EL NO* is a major step in developing our ability to be a greater force for healing and change. Knowing what disempowers us, we can be a more conscious influence to prevent and transform *EL NO* by countering the attitudes and social forces that demean our power, and strengthening our internal concept of self so we can more fully own our power for positive change. We can aid ourselves and others by using co-powering communication to foster positive self-concepts and the attitude of *EL SI*, "Yes, I've got the power!"

Over the years, dozens of people have communicated to me the liberation that resulted for them by coming to understand the dynamic of *EL NO*. They came to realize that they were not inherently stupid, but had been socialized to believe so by negative messages. Awareness of *EL NO* was empowering because they now recognized that their self-doubt did not reflect inherent deficits, but was induced by external influences. Many could trace the origins of

EL NO to early life experiences, or recognized that it was still being reinforced by family or friends knowing no better than to demean others. Regardless, they were now able to discern the internal negative chatter as *EL NO*, and redirect their minds to find ways to support their success.

When I reflect on the transformative power of self-awareness, I recall Lorenzo García, because for him it resulted in dramatic changes in his life. We had an informal conversation at a house party when Lorenzo was in his late twenties. He partied and drank too much, in part from discouragement that he wasn't being the person he wanted to be. In response to the frustration that he confided, I described the dynamics of *EL NO*. He became enthused because it explained why he had been sabotaging his life and also offered him clear choices about his future. In the weeks and months that followed, his new clarity energized him to redirect his life. Lorenzo recalls, "All those years, I felt that it was me who was screwed up. But it wasn't me. It was all those messages of *EL NO* that I swallowed. In retrospect, it seems like common sense, but when you're stuck telling yourself that you're not good enough, you're stuck. You can't recognize your value or see your potential."

Bolstered by new ownership of his power, Lorenzo launched into a new life. He stabilized his financial situation by purchasing and repairing several properties. After a period, this enabled him to pursue what he really wanted to do. He took time to study radio journalism and to commit to several organizing projects. Thirty years later, he admits to periodic struggles with *EL NO*, but the insight that he gained has allowed him to lead a purposeful and successful life. Perhaps his greatest accomplishment has been raising a self-confident and loving daughter who continues the family activist tradition as a fund development consultant for activist organizations.

Lorenzo's story reminds us that we can counter *EL NO* by making our communication with others a source of validation that connects them with their power. Every time we engage in co-powering communication we are advancing cultural transformation by helping develop our collective power to create good for ourselves, our families, and our communities.

Principles for Co-powering Communications

Co-powering is consciously seeking to uplift the confidence and power of others for the mutual good that can result.

When my daughters were young, I would get down on one knee to be at an equal eye level before asking for their thoughts. This was a subtle gesture, yet they received the message—I was validating their worth. As they grew older and their friends would visit, I made time to interact with them, asking about their lives and thoughts. I listened closely and found ways to indicate my respect for their observations and judgments. I was affirming their power, just like my grandmother and several aunts and uncles did for me. As the children became adults, I continued actively listening to understand and demonstrate my respect for them and their ideas. When appropriate, I asked questions to acknowledge their experience and help them discover their own answers. My constant thought was to show them love and validate their power.

For many activists, this may be a radically new way of viewing our responsibility, yet it's necessary. We must counter and transform *EL NO* by continually seeking to lift the confidence and power of

Andrea teaching about success.

everyone around us, particularly our supporters and potential allies. Because we want our children and youth to believe in their intelligence and inner goodness, we also build their self-esteem by validating their experience and judgment. We help reground them to their power by reminding them of their abilities and by reconnecting them to their caring purpose and vision for change.

The ways of co-powering communication are many and only require that you develop your common sense. Begin by asking yourself what type of communications have made you feel more in your power. What did someone do to help boost your *EL SI* or "can do" attitude? Was it the way a person listened to you? Was it what they said and how they said it? Was it the questions they asked or their genuine and kindly feedback?

A survey I conducted among high-achieving Latino university students engaged in community service revealed an interesting insight. When queried about how they developed their self-confidence, almost a third could recall a specific incident when an adult family member, teacher, or coach made eye contact, typically touched them on the shoulder, and said, "I know you can do it." For these young people, this experience either liberated them from *EL NO* or boosted their self-confidence with a heightened awareness that they indeed have the power to achieve their goals.

Reviewing the following list of co-powering principles, and noting those that you currently use and those you can strengthen, can help make you more mindful of the capacity you have for empowering others.

1. **Express love.** Love nurtures self-confidence. Allow yourself to feel that you care about the other person as you communicate. Your intent is to inspire others to love themselves: "I know you're a good person, and you've got my love regardless of the outcome. So, just do it!"

2. **Boost their self-confidence.** Your intent is to assist others to believe in themselves, so be present in a way that communicates your belief in them. Listen closely and share reflections that give them an affirmation of who they are: "That's a great idea. Thanks!"

3. **Support their voice of *EL SI*.** Cultivate within the other a positive attitude of doability, so they know that by applying dedicated effort they can achieve their goals: "I know you have the talent to make it happen, so let's review what you need to do."

4. **Facilitate their connection with purpose.** The greatest gift you can extend to another is assisting them to discover their purpose. Ask questions or provide reflections that aid others to connect with their purpose and thus increase their self-confidence: "I see you interact well with young people. How does this relate to your purpose?"

5. **Recognize their positive attitudes and values.** Provide reflections or ask questions of others that uphold the value of their perspectives and approaches: "I see you as a caring person. You believe in others and this will make you a great teacher."

6. **Remind them of their connection with others.** We have more power when we know we are not alone, so remind others of the support that is available to them: "Remember, just like you have supported us, we are here for you."

Patience and Perseverance

As we practice co-powering communication we can't always expect quick results. With some people our efforts may involve a lifetime of trying and learning. Still, along the way we may save a life or enable someone to become a teacher for the many. I share the story of one of my godchildren.

Rene was not yet two years old, and I was thrilled that his parents trusted me to take him on an outing to the park. As I was walking along the path with Rene on my back, I was already wondering how I could begin teaching this youngster important values and developing his sense of *EL SI*. An idea came to mind, and I began saying hello to every person who passed. I figured that if Rene saw me being friendly and extending hellos, he would learn to trust and extend love to others. When he became a little older, I took him and his brother on neighborhood and country hikes, seeking to make the trips an adventure while developing our relationship and building their self-esteem.

Despite my efforts and the love from his parents, over time Rene found himself on a different path. He was physically small and got into aggressive fighting in school to protect himself. By middle school, his talent for aggression was recognized by older boys and he was recruited by one of the gangs. He soon became a collaborator in their activities and shortly after began his relationship with juvenile hall.

During this period, as Rene became a regular in juvenile institutions, I wrote and visited. In all my communications, I consistently used a five-point strategy—express my love, ask questions to understand his reality, validate his positive qualities, ask questions to help him formulate goals, and share inspiring stories.

To the dismay of his parents and me, juvenile hall time led to doing prison time. Then, during one of his release periods, Rene met a woman he wanted to be with, and his attitude began shifting. I learned about this when I took him out to a Chinese restaurant. I was expecting another of our awkward meal conversations, but this time he talked. He told me about Alice, and with difficulty asked if I could teach him how to order at a restaurant so he could ask her out for a date.

After all these years, I was delighted to have this opening. We talked about relationships, restaurant etiquette, employment interview strategies, and life planning. His relationship with Alice grew, and before long they had a baby. It was inspiring to see Rene be a responsible father. Yet within the year he made a dumb mistake that landed him back in prison. I wrote to him even more than before because I knew him to be good, and his son needed him. The return letters were rare, but I continued to write. I felt he needed to know that I still believed in him.

Over the next few years, Rene separated from his girlfriend and was in and out of prison, struggling with the probation system that failed to recognize and support former inmates earnestly working to be good parents and providers. Finally, the right person, Irma, entered his life, and more than ever Rene committed himself to being a good partner and a good father to both her son and his.

During the last several years, Rene has become a work supervisor, and he and Irma are purchasing their house and making a good home. They live some distance away, and we might only visit once a year, yet the relationship we have established endures. It just takes a phone call and we can easily share about present joys and challenges.

During a conversation last year, Rene confided that he needed help. He loves Irma, but they had gotten into a pattern of arguing. "We're both swearing and saying mean things. I don't want us to live this way because I know it's not good for either of us or the kids." I asked questions to draw out his options while sprinkling in validations about his commitment to family. During our conversation he and I became enthused about him taking action to improve their relationship, agreeing that he was going to talk to Irma about seeing a counselor together. Their conversation led to a dialogue between Irma and me in which I learned that Rene actually had more issues to work on than he initially told me about. He had recently begun drinking too much, which was creating other problems. It was time to make a visit.

After juggling schedules, the three of us were able to meet for breakfast. Responding to my questions, they talked about their expectations for their relationship and family, when the slipups with alcohol arise, what causes the stress, what can be done to prevent or change the unhealthy communication patterns, and more. I also asserted my expectations of both of them as a couple, and specifically of Rene. I told him that I want him to succeed, and I see him capable of eventually being a counselor and role model for young people. He survived the gangs and prison, he has wisdom to impart, and I want him to share it with others.

He heard me, and we heard each other. We ended our short visit with several agreements: Rene would work with a counselor, he and Irma would make time for more communication between them, and we would maintain our communication too. Presently, Rene is doing very well as a responsible partner, father, and work supervisor, and we have begun conversations about how he can use his experience to help young people battle *EL NO* and make decisions to lead healthy lives.

Despite all our positive intentions to develop the self-esteem of our children, some will experience *EL NO* in a way that gets them stuck in behavior patterns that undermine their ability to lead successful lives. At times we will be confronted with the choice of maintaining our support or not. Though it sometimes takes tremendous patience and perseverance to remain supportive through the challenges, I believe we must trust that loving and empowering communication will ultimately lead to positive outcomes.

FAMILY ACTIVISM

PRACTICES

The following are examples of some key family activist practices I employed while supporting Rene:

- Modeling positive values to children
- Seeking to establish relationship and empower young people by expressing love, asking questions, validating positive qualities, and sharing stories that inspire
- Believing in the potential of another, and maintaining a supportive relationship despite challenges
- Being available to coach or counsel
- Proactively maintaining communication
- Challenging the other to fulfill their potential
- Enlisting the support of other family when necessary
- Convening family meetings for problem-solving
- When necessary, urging professional counseling support
- Sharing personal stories of struggle to convey the reality that none of us are perfect and that we are all works in progress

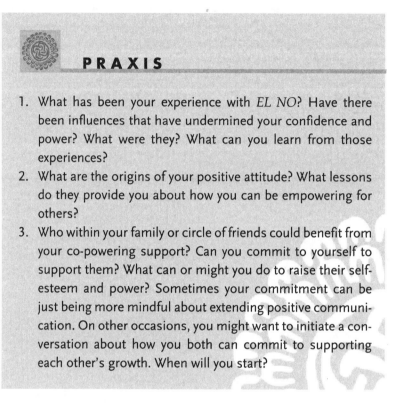

PRAXIS

1. What has been your experience with *EL NO*? Have there been influences that have undermined your confidence and power? What were they? What can you learn from those experiences?

2. What are the origins of your positive attitude? What lessons do they provide you about how you can be empowering for others?

3. Who within your family or circle of friends could benefit from your co-powering support? Can you commit to yourself to support them? What can or might you do to raise their self-esteem and power? Sometimes your commitment can be just being more mindful about extending positive communication. On other occasions, you might want to initiate a conversation about how you both can commit to supporting each other's growth. When will you start?

8

LOVE THE CHILDREN

Boosting family power begins early. We express our love to our young ones and continue to do so through their youth and adulthood. We aid them to grow up self-confident, and inspire them to care for others and our earth. In this process, sharing love, conscious communication, and modeling are our most important tools.

When we look with open wonder at newborn babies, we find that they are absolutely beautiful, intelligent, and courageous. They may wear on you sometimes, or you may feel awkward holding them, yet they already exhibit their brilliance. They know how to move, find comfort, and seek nurturance. In your effort to hold and protect them, you quickly experience their energy and power. Soon they push away to reach out, touch, and discover. These little creatures are full of love and life, and are ready to learn and grow.

Too soon, many of these children experience deficient care from unprepared parents. As much as we love these babies, many of us are so ill informed or overwhelmed that we fail to convey to them how wonderful and brilliant they are. The result is that too many children grow up never knowing or believing in their beauty, intelligence, and potential, and are handicapped by an internal voice of self-depreciation.

To advance a loving society, we must raise our children to believe in their brilliance and *porvida* nature. They need to feel that they are inherent seekers of life, love, and positive living. It is not enough for us to earn the income required to support our family or demand better education for our children. We must also raise and support them to become compassionate and courageous adults—family members and leaders who will take care of themselves, their families, and the next generations. We must raise them with love.

When I say "we," I am not just referring to parents. The "we" is all of us who live in familial or physical proximity to any children, whether it's a nephew, your friend's children, or the kids in your apartment complex. It does take a village to raise healthy children, and we can all accept this as part of our responsibility, making our children feel loved and accepted for the unique individuals they are. All of us can extend to the children in our lives the hugs and caring communication that convey our respect and connection. When we provide them with our unqualified love, their young minds internalize the observation, "If they love me, then I am lovable."

While I feel that I do well in loving my children, I continue to learn, for this is the nature of truly loving. Women like my grandmother and mother have been my role models. They always seem to effortlessly demonstrate their love in the ways they have cared for the children. Their voice, touch, and responsiveness made me feel loved. The combination of their giving ways and my early acceptance that God loved me made me as a five-year-old child feel absolutely bold and courageous. The world was mine to discover and enjoy. I had no reservations about my worthiness or power. Unfortunately, my self-certainty began to erode when I encountered other adults, school, and less idealistic religious teaching. The latter experience is what we want to prevent for our children.

My plea is that as adults we deeply commit to loving our children—all of them, from those we know to any that we meet. We need to actively care for them so that they love themselves, respect life, and own their power. Transforming our world requires thousands and millions of children believing in their purpose and talent. They must come to unquestionably know that they are innately brilliant, and that their purpose is to evolve their ability to love. With caring communication we can facilitate this connection. In turn, these children can help our families to blossom and transform the world.

Start Communicating Early

Communication with our children begins with their birth, if not earlier. I was blessed that while we were expecting our first child a dear friend pulled me aside to offer advice: "As soon as your baby is born, start to get to know him. You don't want to wait, because it gets more complicated later." At the moment I wasn't certain what I would do with this information, but I soon learned.

We were seven weeks short of our due date when Rebeca's temperature rose considerably. Given other pregnancy complications already occurring, our medical advisor told us to immediately get to the hospital. Shortly after arriving we were informed that our baby was in distress, and an immediate cesarean section was required. As soon as the doctor arrived, I made him reaffirm our agreement that whatever happened I was going to stay present with our baby. In the surgery room, as soon as our baby was out, the doctor looked at me and announced, "We've got to run!" He carried her like a football as we ran the length of the corridor and down the steps to intensive care. There, I took over holding our tiny baby while medical staff poked her with one monitoring device after another.

Given our baby's fever and her deformed appearance, the thought entered my mind, "Is she going to be a healthy baby?" I responded to myself that regardless of her appearance or physical handicaps, I was going to love her and I needed to start telling her this now. So I began talking to her—and to God. To God, I requested that this little life be blessed with health, while at the same time I was repeating to our baby that I loved her, her mommy loved her, and we were soon going to take her home and enjoy a great life together.

In the next hour, miracles happened. Her nose straightened out, her arm and head transformed to appear normal, her temperature subsided, and I could see that Rebeca and I were blessed with a healthy baby. At the moment, it felt that the little one and I were talking, laughing, and crying together. I could feel our connection and from then on we have been in constant conversation. We named her Andrea, and I made a life changing commitment. I promised myself

Our children's wisdom, courage, and love will transform the world.

that I was going to be a dedicated *papi*. I was going to raise this little baby to love herself, grow up with confidence, and, ideally, continue our tradition to create justice in the world.

To express my love I spoke to her in Spanish, because this is the language in which I best express love. Every day I would say, *"Mija, sabes cuánto te quiero? Muchísmo!"* (My little sweetheart, do you know how much I love you? Super much!) I wanted her to learn as much about us and the world as possible, so from the time of her infancy I shared about what I was doing and thinking, or about the world, always seeking to use words or ideas that she could grasp.

One of my most inspiring moments occurred a few years later when Andrea was three years old. It was a beautiful sunny day and we had gone to the Berkeley pier for a walk. We were having fun but it was nearing time to leave, so I told her that we had to go because I had to speak to a group of *progente* youth (young people who deeply care for the community). Knowing she was going to hate leaving, I sought to refocus her attention by asking her what I should tell the young people. She took a few moments and said, *"Diles que tienen mucho poder."* Her voice was pensive, yet projected with clear authority, "Tell them they have much power." I was stunned by the profoundness of her comments and quickly pulled out my notebook. I asked, "What else should I say?"

Now, appearing even more confident, she continued, *"Todos tienen corazón. El poder está en el corazón"* (Everyone has heart. The power is in the heart.). As she saw me finish writing one statement she would begin with another, and then another. *"Traten de no pelear."* (Try not to fight.) *"Cuiden el mundo! Todo, todo, todo!"* (Take care of our earth! All of it, all of it, all of it!) *"El poder está en las escuelas y las maestros no deben decir que NO."* (Understand that the power is in the schools and that the teachers should not say NO.) Thrilled at her teachings, I picked her up and swung her around. I thanked her for her advice and told her I would soon be sharing her ideas.

I was amazed at how, at only three years old, she could reflect with such clarity the essence of what we were trying to teach. Our power is in our ability to love. A veteran of only a few months of pre-school and she had already formulated opinions and insights—that fighting shouldn't happen, that we need to remind people to care about others, that there is much to learn at school, and that we need to remind teachers to not be negative.

I was also happy because our pier experience had provided me important feedback on my parenting. We had established a connection, I was doing well, and she was developing her understanding of our *porvida* commitment.

Make Communications Meaningful

Key to my "papihood" (fatherhood) practice is to listen closely, give thoughtful and validating responses, and pose strategic questions. In addition to receiving love, children need to learn to trust their ability to reason, and believe in the worthiness of their questions and reflections. Any question or thought raised by a child is worthy of a thoughtful response. The early questions young children ask are among the most challenging. Why is the sky blue? Where does water come from? How are pencils made? Often, my response is, "Great question. I don't know. What do you think?" or "Let's think about it and then see what answer we can find in the encyclopedia." Today, the resource might be the computer and the Internet.

I asked my children questions while they were preschoolers to assist them in developing their thoughts. Why do you think grandma gets happy when we visit? What did you like about that party? How did that cartoon make you feel? As they answered, I responded with genuine validation of their thoughts, saying, "Interesting," or "Let me share what I like about your thinking," and then communicating my thoughts.

Trust and mutual respect were the main outcomes of these early conversations. We also developed some unhealthy patterns that required attention. Our older daughter was always quick to respond to our questions, often leaving our younger daughter frustrated at her unequal opportunity to share. My wife and I reaffirmed our vigilance to be fair and sensitive regarding this and other patterns, yet still we could have done better.

As the girls grew into their middle school years, I initiated conversations with a combination of what I called my regular and strategic questions. The regular questions sounded like, "What great thing happened today?" or "Did anything difficult happen?" The strategic questions were to help them discover more about themselves, our social reality, and our family's commitment to create a better world: Have you ever thought about being a scientist? If anything was possible, what are three things you would love to do? How can we make this situation better?

The conversations I personally enjoyed most were those about our social reality. Here I asked questions to help them understand cultural pride, prejudice, racism, sexism, capitalism, environmental protection, and social struggle. Of course, we didn't start with conversations about working class exploitation or racism; we began by developing understandings that could enable the deeper conversations. Again, I used questions to facilitate these conversations or created teaching moments to present my ideas on these issues. I was

Pin-the-heart-on-the-President.

elated on those occasions when they did the initiation by putting forth their questions.

When the kids were in first grade we had one of our many birthday parties. Instead of playing pin-the-tail-on-the-donkey, we played pin-the-heart-on-our-President. To introduce the game, I hung up a poster I had made of President Reagan without a heart, and proceeded to explain the power the President has to make decisions that affect our lives. I shared how President Reagan had made decisions that hurt many people. I asked the children why they thought we have homeless people on the street? Validating their responses, I added how many had become homeless when then–California governor Ronald Reagan decided to close the hospitals that mentally ill people needed to get better. "So, maybe he needs more heart. Who wants to play pin-the-heart-on-the-President?" Years later, grown men and women recall how that birthday experience got them to think more critically about all they heard.

During our daughters' elementary school years, we moved from the Oakland flatlands to a white suburban neighborhood. Knowing that the girls would experience many changes due to our departure from the multicultural, bilingual school they loved, we sought to prepare them. We reminded them that the new school was going to include different people and ideas that would make life interesting and adventurous. It did. Soon they were experiencing the subtle and not so subtle prejudice of students and teachers. Rebeca and I decided on a multi-prong approach. We saw that we needed to educate the teachers and make presentations to the classrooms, as well as continue discussions with our children.

In our conversations with our daughters, we invited them to express their feelings, using questions like, "How did it make you feel when you heard kids say that you are not like other Mexicans?" We shared about prejudice and how it develops. We explained how prejudice occurs when people don't have the opportunity to learn about other people. Because of our discussions, the girls finished elementary school with a clear understanding of the dynamics of prejudice and social struggle, and realized it is our family responsibility to inform and educate others.

Be the Uncle or Aunt for the Many

When we extend love and respect to our children, it is relatively easy to extend similar feelings to the surrounding children. While you are interacting to build the confidence of your child, nephew, or niece, you can also lift the self-esteem of her or his friends. If you are being the loving dad or mom for one, you can just as easily be the adult friend, uncle, or aunt for the others.

As our children were growing up, I established my office at the house and we made our home the after-school hangout. It took a few excursions to garage sales to collect all we needed to create a space where youngsters could visit to do their homework and have fun. We set up the extra computer, several encyclopedia sets, and a ping-pong table. The main rules were that all visiting kids had to stop by and say hello to me first, had to spend at least an hour or so on homework, and then they could hang out.

Given the rapport I developed with our young visitors, it was not uncommon for one or two to stop by my office and ask if I might take a break to play ping-pong or Frisbee. Sometimes the offer was simply to play, and other times it was a code indicating the desire to talk. The conversations could be about alcohol, dating, difficult parents, life goals, or even national and world issues. Regardless of the topic, every dialogue presented an opportunity to lift these youngsters up and for me to experience the joy of interacting with young people.

Sometimes we may consider setting aside time to engage with young people as a chore because it takes us away from other tasks or priorities. But it can just as well be a time of magic during which you witness the impact of extending love. My fondest of such memories is the campout we planned for my godchildren.

I am formally and informally godparent to eight young people. I take my godparent responsibility seriously and do my best to maintain our relationship. One year, feeling disappointed that I hadn't spent time with most of them, I consulted with Rebeca and we decided to bring them all together for a holiday dinner gathering. Besides reconnecting with them, I envisioned the potential of several of them meeting others for the first time and developing relationships of mutual support.

Because being a godfather to one is also like being an uncle to their brother or sister, we had thirteen young people from thirteen to twenty-one years old join us for the gathering. Everyone was asked to come early to help me wrap white sage leaves into bundles for our use in future ceremonies, then to share in a ceremony circle, and later enjoy dinner together.

When it came time for the ceremony, which was a "gratitude circle," everyone sat on our living room floor around a simple altar comprised of candles and the sage we had wrapped. After lighting the candles and one of the sage bundles, we opened with a prayer in which everyone was invited to express their words of gratitude. Afterward, I asked that each take a turn to share something about themselves so the others would know them better, and why they had chosen to come this evening. Most of our guests only knew a couple of the others, but given the trust that was felt during the circle, several expressed deep truths about their personal struggles.

Amidst the sharing, one of the young people asked me what occurs at the retreats I do for adults and organizations. I explained that I create situations where people can express their problems or hopes, and then we work on resolutions. One of them reflected, "Then, it's something like what we are doing now?" Then the question arose whether I would organize a retreat for them, "just us and not our parents." A dialogue ensued in which I ultimately agreed to explore organizing a godchildren's retreat, with the understanding that they would abide by my retreat plan.

Their enthusiasm excited me, and I approached my brother Art to see if he would help. Art doesn't have children, but has always been a great uncle to my children and someone I often turn to for assistance. We projected a date six weeks later for a two-night retreat at a local camping area.

The first evening of the retreat, we set up camp, and the program started the next morning at breakfast. I presented my hope for all of them—to lead good and successful lives, and to continue our tradition of giving back to our families and community. I briefly elaborated that success in life requires that we learn how to develop relationships of trust and mutual support. This retreat was going to be about practicing these ideals.

My instructions for the young people were as follows: During the course of the day, they could do whatever they desired, such as fishing, swimming, hiking, or anything else. They just had to share a conversation with at least two other people in which each would respond to several questions that I had written out on *conocimiento* cards: (1) What do you like best about yourself? (2) What do you like best about your family? (3) What goals do you have for yourself or your family? I told them that we were going to have a campfire in the evening and discuss what we had learned.

We were blessed with a beautiful day and evening. Everyone did their connecting, and the campfire dialogue began with the young folks sharing what they had discovered about each other, and the difficulty they had experienced in talking about their good qualities. Conversing about the best aspects of their families quickly shifted to dialogue about the struggles several were having with their parents. I halted the discussion to ask if this was an area everyone felt we should go into. The response was that if a person felt she or he needed to talk about a problem, it should be okay. I agreed, if we first talked about the meaning of confidentiality. We did this and collectively agreed that everything shared was not to be repeated.

While the discussion that evening did not go too much deeper, we all learned from each other. By the time we finished we all had a greater respect for *familia*, what it meant, what it required, and how fortunate we were to have our families. Reflecting on the entire time together, I felt we accomplished much good. We had created a memorable experience for my daughters and the godchildren—for a couple of days we were an extended family enjoying each other and learning how to be better family members.

This story illustrates at least two key ideas. First, we owe it to ourselves and the children to make quality sharing time one of our priorities, so we can support their growth and they ours. Second, there are an infinite number of ways for sharing quality time with young people, from organizing a semi-structured retreat to something as simple as extending an invitation for a shared walk. Treat our young friends like family and we change the world.

It's Never Too Late

Many parents ask, is it ever too late to establish a real connection with your children? I say no, but it does take faith, persistence, and good fortune. Faith here is an optimism that the connection can happen. As activists we must keep trying our best while learning from our experience.

Love is actively caring for another. It is built on our ability to develop a connection with others that welcomes the ongoing expression and exchange of feelings and thoughts. With our youth, this involves developing a relationship in which they feel trust and even joy sharing about life, including the difficult issues. Evolving and experiencing this level of exchange is living love, but it is easier to adopt as a goal than to accomplish.

With my first daughter, the expression of love and our easy back-and-forth communication seemed to evolve naturally and easily. With our second daughter, Cheli, I discovered that children are different and how challenging developing a relationship of communication can be. After years of trying and coming close to giving up, I finally came to several realizations. I should not be so judgmental, enjoy the exchanges we do have, and be freer in expressing love. I also recognized that we both have more learning to do, and that we have time to make it happen.

We must remember that every child is uniquely different. Some enjoy communication more than others. Some welcome your counsel, and others seek to learn about life in their own way. Some prefer talking with peers rather than parents. From the time Cheli was a child, she seemed to favor less communication, at least with me. My challenge was to accept her for who she was, and not be so quick to see her independent behavior as rejection. She was doing what she should, asserting her own personality.

While communications flowed with Andrea during her preteen and teen years, interacting with Cheli was a struggle. Our timing was always off. Every time I initiated a conversation it seemed to be the wrong content or time. Was the issue my expectations or her rebellion given the greater attention she felt her sister received? My wife and I talked about it and recognized it was true that Andrea often asserted herself in a way that generated more attention. So, to connect with Cheli, I consciously tried multiple strategies. I created one-to-one time, responded to her interests, extended praise, and engaged with her friends. Still, I always felt limited success. Out of frustration, I periodically required her to talk with me, which often resulted in her tears, which in turn elicited from me greater frustration and anger. All this, of course, usually resulted in setbacks in our relationship.

I continued trying during her high school years, and as her graduation neared it seemed that we had run out of time. Yet, as she departed for college I held a hope that maybe her living some distance away would help us evolve a deeper level of communication. But, although we stayed in touch, I still didn't feel the quality of connection I hoped for. After receiving her degree, Cheli returned home, and I hoped this would be our time to make the connection. Several months later I felt we were nearing a threshold of new possibilities, when she announced that she was moving away to "do her own life."

I was hurt and upset. Actually, I felt I had failed. Communication was still difficult, and she was not being the activist I had envisioned. Instead of enjoying the remaining time before her departure, I was making it difficult for everyone with my attitude. Fortunately, I woke up in the middle of one night with a head full of insights. I realized that just because she was moving did not mean my effort would end, and, most important, that I should feel proud that she is a wonderful, self-confident, and caring person pursuing her own path. I also realized how much I had inadvertently imposed my ideas of activism and successful communication upon our relationship. What about her ideas and her vision? It was time to enjoy and support the person she had become, while remaining open to growing our relationship.

Since then, our relationship has evolved to a new maturity. Cheli has connected more with her own power and courage. Through our conversations, she has enlightened me about her experience of me, someone who—to a child—could be scary and have an ill temper. Rather than bringing out the best in me, her childhood tears often brought out the worst, as they unconsciously triggered within me a sense of failure. So rather than responding with increased sensitivity to her tears, my vivid frustration only served to drive us further apart. I have only begun to understand this, but I recognize that she is now providing me consultation on how to be a better parent and communicator.

As a parent and activist, it is essential to maintain balance. Extend love, receive love, and be love. Teach love, accept love, and be open to the unique ways our children will accept, reflect, and integrate these lessons. Model, teach, be present, listen, and be continually open to learn from our children and all young people. At times, our best students will not be our own children, but others ready for or needing a caring adult in their lives. In any case, continue supporting the children, trusting that they will return to you and the world the love they receive.

PRAXIS

1. What has been your experience of receiving love from family and friends? How was it expressed? How have you benefited from this love?
2. How do you currently express love within your family, to your partner, children, parents, and friends? How might you improve your ability for communicating or sharing love? Note in your journal the ideas you take from these questions to assist you to better communicate your love.
3. Select one of the sections of this chapter and read it to family and friends. Ask them what insights or lessons surfaced for them, and how might they apply these insights within their relationships.

9

LEARN, COMMUNICATE, AND TEACH

● ●

Our desire is heaven on Earth, a society in which people actively care for each other, schools support our children to become their best, government serves the will of the people, and corporations act on behalf of the common good. To create such a society requires tremendous amounts of communication, learning, and teaching.

Know the Reason for Your Communication

As family activists, it's important to realize both the enormous influence we wield via our communications and the significance of knowing the purpose of our communication. Every day we engage in dozens of communications. We communicate to express a good morning greeting, to coordinate the day's activities, and sometimes to offer feedback to others about what's working or not working. Yet, how often do we stop to consider the powerful influence of our communications—not just what we say, but why and how we say it? Our communication can lift self-esteem, inspire, teach, or it can reinforce a sense of apathy and powerlessness. It's our choice. Given the evolving crises in our world, it's time to learn to make our communication as impactful as possible so as to enhance the power of family and friends to become greater contributors to transformation.

Toward this end, it is imperative to communicate with purpose in mind—to foster self-love, lift self-esteem, facilitate connection, teach, and assist others to discover their power to advance positive change for themselves and others. Regardless of a person's age, what's important is to cultivate that person's ability to be caring, courageous, and people-connected. Keeping this intention in mind will make your communication more effective.

Most of us think of communication as words conveying our message, but the reality is that much of our communication is nonverbal. Dr. Albert Marabian's classical study in communication determined that 7 percent of meaning is conveyed in the words that are actually spoken, 38 percent in the way the words are delivered, and 55 percent by facial expression.[1] In any face-to-face communication, we unconsciously communicate to others what we feel and think largely by a combination of facial expressions and body language. For this reason, it's important to be grounded in our purpose when we communicate. When wishing to convey love or to empower, you become more effective in achieving your desired outcome when your body, spirit, and strategy are aligned to your intent.

Alignment means that everything said and done is consistent with and conveys your message. So if your intent is to empower a family member or friend, this is how you might approach it. First, you remind yourself, "Right now, my intention is to make my friend feel her power." Then get in touch with your genuine positive feelings for this person. Whether your feelings arise from an interest to know her better or from deep caring, get in touch with that feeling so it becomes what you emanate. From this place, open yourself to sense who she is and what she may need in the moment. Her need may be for someone to truly listen to her current challenge, or maybe provide a simple acknowledgement or just a "pick-me-up." Grounding yourself in your purpose and taking a few moments to connect with her needs, you will usually know what to do next. Maybe she needs a couple of strategic questions to help her reconnect with her power or provide a simple reminder of her intelligence. Often, you can be empowering just by listening, because it conveys that you care.

The other day, a *compadre* called, and while I assumed it was a business-related call, I soon realized he was a friend in need. I took a breath to connect more to my heart, and listened. He is dean of a school and, given evolving challenges, he was questioning whether he should muscle up and deal with the new difficulties or consider leaving his job. While my personal interest is to see him continue as dean, I reminded myself to consider him as a person I really care about. I focused on truly listening to him, and in so doing I faintly heard his deeper desire that led me to ask him several questions, such as "Are you living your purpose?" "Are you happy?" Hearing his own responses, he connected with his power to make the decisions ultimately best for himself and for others.

Reconnecting with my purpose to be a supportive and empowering friend, I was able to identify and then ask the real questions my *compadre* needed to consider. Even over the phone, he could feel my respect and support for him. Because of the integrity between my words and the energy I conveyed, he was able to both hear and feel my appreciation of his capacity for insight. It helped him acknowledge and validate his power to access his wisdom and find his own answers.

The more we practice remaining mindful of our purpose as we communicate, aware of our feelings for the other, and fully present, the more we learn to trust and guide our communications toward that purpose. We learn to listen more deeply and allow the needs of the other to inform us of how to be co-powering.

Learning About Love

Our ultimate goal is to foster a culture of love in which people genuinely care about and serve each other. To teach such compassion begins by maturing in our own ability to love. This is a lifelong process which demands that we repeatedly remind ourselves to work toward our best. For this reason, we need to continually help each other to discover and remain on the path of love. The story of my own maturation involves both assisting others and needing assistance from others.

My motivation for community betterment grew out of my childhood experience of receiving love. During my early twenties, the source of my inspiration shifted, in part due to my encounters with prejudice and racism. Beginning in high school and through my college years, the occasions on which I had to deal with people belittling me or yelling at me for being a "Mexican" increased. Anger and a desire for justice became my stronger motivations. As ugly encounters with racism continued, I became still angrier, but I learned to use my anger to psych myself up to work longer and harder to combat it. Unfortunately, in so doing, I also developed and fueled my own prejudice.

Without realizing it, I had started to sound like the people who had injured me. My venting about the disrespect inflicted upon me and those of my community became more frequent and critical of the character of all white people. Then one day I was stunned by my younger brother, Marcos, who courageously confronted me with his love. He said that despite having viewed me as his role model for years, he could no longer listen to me because I was too full of hate. My initial reaction was anger at him. Couldn't he see all the good that I was doing? Yet, over many days, as I cooled down I recognized that I had become consumed by my anger. I realized it was time to consciously reprogram my motivation, not to deny my experiences with injustice and racism, but to nurture my original inspiration, which was love.

Thirty years later, I still work on being loving in all my actions. I see this as fundamentally a contest between my selfish nature and my giving nature, and I know the mature side is winning. For many of us, being a loving person takes practice, reflection, patience, and more practice and reflection. It takes asking, "How can I be more giving to others in each communication?" and then following through. Periodically, it involves telling yourself, "I did great!" After a while, it becomes a habit and way of being. A conversation a short while ago with my mother provided me additional insight about teaching love.

One day I observed a dramatic increase in my mom's energy and physical facility when we received a surprise visit from her young granddaughters. Shortly before, I had seen her painfully struggle to move, yet upon their arrival, she had outstretched arms inviting these youngsters to stampede her with their joy. Soon after, she was preparing their favorite meal. It made me wonder, and later I asked her about this: "The love I see you exhibit in your actions, where does it come from, your mind or heart?" Roughly translated from

Spanish, she responded, "It just flows because that's who I am. If it weren't for the love inside me, I don't think I could even get up in the morning. Maybe I think about it a little—like how I can serve my family today—but later the love just moves me." Our conversation continued, and I explained that while I feel love for my nieces, I usually have to recognize my feelings for them and then think about what I might do to express my love. I feel first, think, and then act. That's what prompts me to invite them to play a game so we can connect, talk, and have some fun, while I also seek opportunities to support their growth.

This conversation got me to evaluate my actions more. Maybe for some of us, by virtue of our own psychology and experience, our acts of love do just flow. I seem to observe this more among women than among men. For others, like me, who still seem to be learning about being loving, we are more directed by the "feel, think, and then act" approach. In the final analysis, both caring types can benefit by developing greater mindfulness of our teacher role to advance love. Why? Because the love we need to transform our society involves both—the flow of the deep heartfelt hugs and the mindful consideration committed to helping others develop. We need both and much more. To transform our society requires people who possess self-love, impart that love unconditionally, and also have the confidence and ability to create change within themselves, their relationships, and all our institutions. Toward this end, we must always be ready and constant learners and teachers of love.

Empower by Providing Experiences that Inspire

We communicate not only through what we convey in words, but by the experiences we create for others that inform and inspire them. Dolores Huerta, nationally recognized civil rights leader and parent of eleven children who are also activists, recently shared with me her key strategy for empowering.[2] She said, "As organizers we develop people's self-confidence just by getting them to a meeting or rally. We tell them, Just be there. Just come to the march. Just come to the rally. Just come to the meeting and bring your kids. The experience will empower them and their kids."

In preparing to write this book, I interviewed dozens of activists to ask what influenced their caring commitment, and also asked many parents how they sought to foster an activist spirit in their children. What they shared were essentially three key strategies: conversations, storytelling, and providing experiences that expressed the dynamics of hardship, struggle, and love. Here I convey the types of experiences we can create to inspire and motivate our children.

Create Learning Conversations

Kapua Sproat, an environmental advocacy attorney and law professor, belongs to an extended family strongly involved in fostering native Hawaiian culture, building native Hawaiian institutions, and advocating for native Hawaiian rights.[3] Kapua says her parents simply used the "meet, visit, and picket sign approach." Her parents took their children to all community meetings, visits, and protests. The children learned to care by observing and participating in activism, and through the conversations of family and friends at the dinner table. Similarly, many activists developed their caring commitment by observing, accompanying, and helping their parents as they aided neighbors, made their homes available to others, engaged in church activities to serve the community, registered voters, or organized protests. The young people directly saw the need, heard the stories of social struggle, witnessed people taking action, and they joined in.

Many other activists are like Patricia Loya, who was inspired by the stories she heard around the kitchen table. Her parents came from an Arizona mining community where her father was a copper miner. "At dinner, he would tell us about when he used to work at the mines, the dangerous working conditions, and the racist treatment of Mexican workers. But he'd also tell us what he and others were doing to make a difference. Sometimes the stories would be about workers getting hurt or even killed. I'd be angry and upset, but also felt pride because he was always organizing to make conditions better." Later, her parents became teachers and advocates for farm workers and youth, which brought even more people into their living room. "We saw them organizing, planning, and laughing, and as kids, we wanted to get involved too." Hearing the stories of injustice and efforts for change, and witnessing the activist work up close, encourages young people to care for others and commit to "giving back." Now, both Patricia and her sister are directors of major community legal assistance centers doing tremendous advocacy work on behalf of immigrant workers.[4]

I still recall the cold December evening when our minister asked me to accompany him to deliver blankets to people living in our church's neighborhood. I can still see the young mother cooking over an open pit stove on the dirt floor of a makeshift lean-to no larger than a small cave. After that evening, I felt blessed to be living in comfort, and I also felt responsible to make a difference for those struggling to survive. That evening, Reverend Rodriquez communicated a lesson about service to me without saying a word.

We can impart knowledge and nurture a caring spirit to develop activists by modeling, asking questions, sharing activities, and facilitating conversations. When I visited my uncle who was recovering from diabetes-related surgery, I started a conversation with his nephews who were present. We teach by affirming and complementing the knowledge possessed by others, so our conversation mainly involved my raising a sequence of questions, their responses, my elaboration, and more questions. Do you know what diabetes is? Why do you think Uncle got sick? What do you think about television commercials that encourage us to eat sugar-laden foods that undermine our health? What can we do to protect ourselves and others from getting diabetes? What can we do to make Uncle proud? By the time we finished our conversation, a couple of the young people reaffirmed their commitment to study and find ways to make a difference for their family and community.

Bring Home the Storytellers

Many of the lessons we need to learn or desire to teach about community service and social struggle are not taught by lectures, but by stories. When a real-life story is delivered, we often deeply listen because it involves someone's life experience. Then it is up to us to garner the lessons, or our interest may have been so piqued that we have many questions to ask and a learning conversation ensues. We

We can inspire others by sharing our experience and stories. Compadre Jerry encourages creative activism by relating his own rich experiences.

should all consider developing our ability for storytelling, particularly those stories that can teach others about our social conditions, struggles, and victories to create the changes we desire. Meanwhile, spending time with storytellers is always worthwhile and the best way to cultivate this talent in yourself.

My regular counsel to young people is to wait to find the right person with whom to create a life partnership. For me this has made a tremendous difference in my activism, as Rebeca has been a fantastic partner and collaborator in supporting many of the family practices important to me, including making our home available not only for family, but for friends and others who might need a place to stay.

Despite living in a small two-bedroom house in Oakland, I can't recall a time when we didn't have people staying with us for short or long periods. Our visitors were students new to the area without a place to stay, friends experiencing challenges and needing a supportive environment, friend-of-friend activists visiting the area, and others. I thoroughly enjoyed welcoming visitors, simply to offer the comfort of our home, and also for the feeling of *familia* that occurs as we share life and stories. This became more significant during the early years of our daughters' lives when I realized that every one of our visitors could be a teacher for them. When visitors asked how they could help, my request would be for them to tell us some stories about their lives or activist work. Over the years, we heard many stories that served to teach and inspire us.

Late one evening, I received a telephone call from the receptionist of a community center for which I had recently begun working. I had only shared a couple of conversations with Linda, but as she was a Native American sister struggling to survive in San Francisco, I had given her my card with the offer to call me if she ever needed support. Now she told me that she didn't have time to talk, it was a matter of life or death, she needed to move out of her room immediately, and she needed a place to stay. My gut response was to offer support, so upon finishing the call I told Rebeca, a friend needs a place to stay and I have to go get her. It's an emergency and I will explain when I return.

A couple of hours later, I returned with Linda, who was very grateful but also petrified with fear. Over the course of the next couple of days, her story unfolded. As a youngster she and her siblings had been virtually made indentured workers on an Oklahoma farm. She ran away a number of times, and every time she was found and locked in a windowless room for increasingly more days and weeks. Consequently, she developed an overwhelming fear of closed spaces. Years later in Colorado a well-to-do gentleman attempted to rape her in a park. She ultimately fended him off by striking him with his cane. Later, he was able to use his privileged status to have her charged with assault. With the prospect of several years in jail, Linda skipped bail and had been living underground. The night she called me, she was certain that she was about to be arrested.

Linda had other stories of the deplorable ways Native Americans are still treated in this country. During the several weeks she stayed with us, besides helping in the kitchen, my only request was that she share her stories with my children. Through her storytelling we became more sensitive to the realities of her people, and healing occurred for her as she was able to relate her experiences.

When we selected our next home, we all wanted to have an extra room for guests. We continued to hear stories from many visitors. As a result, we learned how to better support people with AIDS, about the struggles of young people, the power of art in activist work, organizing activity occurring in different parts of the county, and much more.

Learning to Be an Advocate

Life can bring unexpected experiences that teach us and our families tremendous lessons of contradiction, courage, learning, and change. This happened for my family and me when our lives were radically altered by the molestation of our daughter Andrea. The story of our experience is shared to remind us of the great courage and ongoing conversations and learning that are often required to care for and heal our own families. It is also intended to inspire us as family activists to truly be advocates for our families, our own children and other children, and to find forgiveness.

For me, the story begins when Carl and I lived together as roommates. We were a perfect match, not just because we were attending the same graduate program, committed to cleanliness, and politically compatible, but also because our work styles complemented each other. I held a vision of a better world and was driven every day to organize and work toward that end. Carl shared a similar vision, yet also believed in enjoying life. We developed a mode of collaboration based on his proviso of balance, which meant that periodically we made time for music, fishing, and having the boys over for drinks and cards.

For the next couple of years we were a powerful team assisting various communities in their organizing efforts. Our relationship became even more like family after Rebeca and I had our own home with two young toddlers, and Carl came to live with us off and on for several years. It was great. Carl was excellent with kids, so our daughters had an uncle in the house, my wife had a trusted friend, and I had an older brother, a colleague, and a comrade in the struggle.

Several years later, our ideal family life changed forever. Carl was no longer living with us, but was a frequent visitor to our home. One weekend evening, we were enjoying a great dinner gathering when Carl informed me that he had to leave. Because I wanted his consultation on several projects, I insisted that he stay a little longer, but he finally convinced me to let him go. After our final guests left, Rebeca asked that I join her in my office because there was something we had to talk about. She described to me what had occurred. Andrea, who was then ten years old, had invited her beloved uncle to see her newly decorated play house that I had made for her under the family room stairway. Once in that tiny room he fondled her and tried to French-kiss her, while blocking her exit. She finally squeezed away and in shock ran to Rebeca.

After hearing this, we joined our daughters in their room, and Andrea now told me what happened. I didn't want to believe her. My immediate thoughts were, "Impossible, Carl could never do anything like this. Impossible!" Yet also echoing in my mind were the stories I had heard from at least half a dozen women who said that the worst part of their molestation had been when their parents had not believed them. It took all my inner strength to restrain myself from asking, "Are you sure this happened?" and to instead say, "*Mija*, I'm so sorry. It's not your fault, and we are never going to let this happen again."

I saw the fear in her eyes as she said, "But, Papi, he has a key to our house. What if he comes back?" My thoughts were, "F--k you, Carl! How could you do this to her, to me, to us?" As much as I didn't want to believe what I was about to say, I pulled her close and told her not to worry—he would never come back to our house.

After we put the girls to bed, Rebeca filled me in with the details. She had been working in the kitchen when she turned to see Andrea ghostly pale, breathing hard and perspiring. After hearing what had occurred, she comforted Andrea and tried to reassure her of her safety. Rebeca then confronted Carl, who denied that anything had happened. It was a misunderstanding, he said. Rebeca told him that there was no misunderstanding and she demanded he immediately leave the house. For the sake of our other guests, she thought it best to wait until everyone had left before telling me. She wanted to kill him.

The next morning, I called Carl, not knowing what I was going to say, but knowing that I needed to meet with him directly and soon. He began by arguing that it was just a misunderstanding. I told him to stop and listen, "If you are still into denying what happened, then you are sicker than you realize. I want to meet with you now."

Forty-five minutes later, I arrived at his apartment. When he answered his door, the first words were an apology. "You're right. I really messed up. I'm so sorry. I don't deserve to be part of your family. I know you have to do what you have to do. And if it's going to the police, let's just do it now." Pushing into his apartment, I said, "I don't want to go the police. I want to know how could you do this to Andrea? To all of us? We've been family. Why did you f--k it up for all of us?"

We talked. I wanted to be angrier. I wanted to lose control and punch him out. But mostly I was sad. Sad for him because I knew our family made him whole. And as much as I wanted to be angry for Andrea, I was sad for myself. I was losing my brother and chief collaborator. Selfishly, I thought, Andrea has our love and will recover, but how am I going to continue without Carl?

He expressed his shame. The day of the party he had been drinking before arriving at our home, and he had just lost it. As he spoke, I was visualizing the future and struggling with what would come next. I thought, "In three or four months, he could complete a treatment program and the family could forgive him. Damn, I need his support." We were inspiring young people, creating community, and developing activist leaders. What was I going to tell our colleagues? Our friends? The community? Then I remembered that for Andrea, he had to see that I was angry and adamant. I asked for my keys and told him I wanted to hear that he was seeing a counselor within the week.

For the next several weeks, the girls needed comforting, and it was provided. We mostly spoke with Andrea, as Cheli didn't want to talk about it. I made calls to find counseling services for Andrea, which led to the county's Child Protective Services interviewing everyone in our household. They determined that we had responded well, and that both girls appeared to be fine. They did not, unfortunately, provide us any insight about how this experience would continue impacting our family over the rest of our lives.

The following months were challenging. First, we struggled with whom to inform about Carl. Here was one of our community leaders, a man recognized and respected by many for his community service. To announce his violation to the world seemed wrong, yet some explanation of his alienation from us was necessary. This was compounded by Andrea's insistence that we not tell people what had happened. She didn't want to live with the embarrassment. We negotiated a strategy. We decided to inform only those closest to our family about what happened, particularly those families with children. For most others, when the question arose, there was just an awkward statement that we were no longer relating.

Soon after, Andrea courageously put forth a request: "Papi, I feel scared when your men friends come to the house. Can you just ask them to stop coming over?" My initial impulse was to respond that she was asking too much—after all, these were good people, they were not Carl. But I caught myself and we talked. I agreed that I would have fewer men visiting the house. I also expressed my trust in her intuition. If she ever felt uncomfortable about any of our visitors, she was free to leave the room and we could talk about it later.

Compounding the situation, arguments and tension arose with my younger brother, Art. Over the years, he had grown to respect Carl and also saw him as family. Having no children himself, his feeling was that there needed to be a consideration of the degree of the molestation, since it wasn't rape. His view was that Carl was sick, needed help, and we should be more open to work with him and forgive. I repeatedly felt angry with Art because his sensitivity seemed directed more to Carl than to Andrea. For the most part, we elected not to bring up further conversation around this issue.

At the same time, I truly did want to forgive Carl. I knew he had seen a counselor, and I heard that his weekly poker nights were now alcohol-free. This was a radical change. Enthused about these developments, I raised the question to my family whether there was a possibility of forgiving Carl. The unanimous reaction was "No!" with my wife giving me a sound lashing for even considering the possibility. Yet I continued to consider it over the next several years, until another molestation surfaced. This time it involved another community leader, Pete, and his grandniece, the niece of one of our dear friends.

During the subsequent weeks, I thought hard and deep about this issue of child molestation. I began to wonder if we had made a mistake by hushing up the actions of these men. Does this type of behavior continue because men do not want to lose their friends, because men do not make public our judgment about what is wrong? Was I going to be silent about Pete's behavior as well?

I shared my thoughts with Andrea, who was now sixteen years old. I told her that I believed it was important that we participate in being a voice that says that the molestation of children is wrong and will not be tolerated. She asked with whom I wanted to share her experience. I told her that I wanted to begin with the men's council that I had belonged to for the past twelve years. Her request was that for the time being, I only share with them.

The result was one of our council's most difficult gatherings. Some had known about Carl, but the news about Pete was a shock for everyone. Of course, the question arose, can we know for certain? Do we know if his niece is telling the truth? I shared how similar my reactions were when my daughter told me about Carl. We don't want to believe our respected peers are capable of such behavior, and we first want to protect them rather than consider the child. I asked, when are we going to believe our children and denounce this violent behavior by our peers?

Before the end of the evening, a couple of members of our group shared how they had been victimized as children. One shared how his experience led him to make it his life's work to educate men about our need to change that part of our culture that perpetuates this form of violence. We didn't arrive at a final resolution, but we all left with an increased awareness that there are issues of dysfunction among men that must be addressed. Also, we realized that it may be time to become more vigilant, to raise the issue, and confront each other about abuse.

Since then, another molestation has surfaced within our circle of extended family. This time, we have become active advocates for the child. My wife, daughter, and I have spoken to the perpetrator, informing him that we know about the situation and that our alliance is absolutely with his daughter. Hearing his remorse, our commitment remains with his daughter, and secondarily to support him in revealing his act to others as a means of preventing further harm to his child and others.

As a family, our own healing around our Andrea's experience with molestation is still incomplete. As individuals, each of us still carries personal wounds, and as a family we are growing to believe that a more complete closure may not occur until Carl hears directly from us the trauma caused by his actions. We are learning that communication and truth are essential, accountability is necessary, change and forgiveness are possible, and the layers of hurt, discovery, and healing sometimes require a lifetime.

I share this story for several reasons. First and foremost, from the core of my being, I don't want to hear of another child being molested. Just as we must stop the violence of guns, exploitation, and war, we must stop the violence inflicted against children and women. While we may have less influence to halt the former, we are often in a position to confront the violence that happens within families around us. I also want people to realize that family activism is at times about directly addressing the hard issues, by confronting wrongdoing and being advocates for the vulnerable. This sometimes requires us to make our family issues community issues.

In agreeing to make this story public, Andrea asked that it end with her appeal that each person reading it share it with at least one other, with the question, "What can be done to better protect our children?" She also asks that each person commit to discuss any abuse they may be aware of, rather than keeping silent.

PRAXIS

1. What strategies might you use to foster the caring spirit or the social consciousness of the children or young people in your family network? Initiate a one-to-one, or a session with a couple of young people, in which you ask them how you might be able to help other youth develop their sense of caring for others and for the earth.

2. Reflecting on what inspired your initial activism or what inspires you now, identify a story or experience you could share with others to inform or inspire them about the importance of activism or community service. Develop your story and find an opportunity to share it with your family or friends.

3. Reflecting on the story of the molestation, what would you do regarding the perpetrator if you were the child's parent? The uncle or aunt? What do you believe should be done when the perpetrator is your close friend or family? What can you do for the young people you know to protect them from such violence?

10

BE THE FACILITATOR

●●●●●●●●●●●●●●●●●●●●●●●●●●●●●●●●●●●●●●

The most powerful skill that activists can possess is the ability to bring people together to share meaningful conversation. Every day the need or opportunity arises to assist a group to plan, solve problems, have fun, or to share caring thoughts. When we know how to convene these groups and guide their conversation so that everyone participates, we can make major contributions to their transformation. The skill of assisting groups to effectively converse and work together is called group facilitation, and it is an essential tool in family activism.

I have been facilitating family gatherings for more than thirty-five years, as a son, brother, father, and a friend to many families. The first meetings I facilitated were to help restore unity within my family, then to coordinate our family response to the challenges that came later, including caring for my father after a disabling surgery and supporting my mother after his death. By the time our oldest child was four years old, my wife and I had developed the tradition of holding spontaneous and regular family meetings to plan and coordinate our lives. The skills I developed coupled with my desire to support other families led me to become a regularly invited facilitator for the gatherings of friends, particularly when they were hosting major celebrations involving many families.

I love facilitating all types of meetings and gatherings. I enjoy witnessing the growth that can occur and partaking in the feelings of pride and achievement when we end with clear accomplishments. I believe we all can develop our skills to either facilitate or support effective family conversations, meetings, and gatherings. It will take commitment, some courage, and then experience to fully develop your skill, yet while you are learning you can be assisting your family to better take care of itself.

My exposure to meetings began underneath our kitchen table, where I would play with cars or soldiers while my mother and others met above taking care of church business. Here I learned that people meet to get things done. My discovery of the power of meetings occurred later, when I joined the Boy Scouts shortly before my eleventh birthday. My first assignment was to meet with three other kids to plan an upcoming campout for the troop of maybe three dozen scouts. With the guidance of our patrol leader, my fourteen-year-old cousin John Pineda, we met on a Saturday afternoon to plan the activities, meals, equipment needs, and assignments for the trip. A couple of weeks later, when I was experiencing the best outdoor outing of my life, I reflected on the planning we had done to make this all happen. I was amazed at how an hour meeting had resulted in such a coordinated and fun experience. I then became super-curious about how meetings worked.

For the next dozen years, my observation of meetings mostly taught me how meetings don't work because most people have never been taught how to guide them effectively. They do their best with what they informally pick up, and I learned enough this way to guide me in organizing and operating several counseling centers. Then, fortunately, I took a social work course in which one of the required books was *How to Make Meetings Work*.[1] Finally, after many years, I was exposed to the language and technology of meeting facilitation.

"Facilitation" comes from the Latin word *facil*, meaning "to make easy." One of the chief responsibilities of a facilitator is to make the work of participating in conversations or meetings easy and meaningful. The facilitator serves the group by supporting the full participation of all members toward achieving the group's goals. This knowledge was empowering because it provided me with a framework to translate my evolving group experience into an organized set of skills for working with all groups. My mantra became, "Be the facilitator!"

With ever-increasing confidence in my facilitation skills, I was always ready to suggest to any group of people, "Let's get together and figure it out." While the technology of facilitation was mostly developed for work groups, my main interest became facilitating meetings for families and community groups. For these groups, my objective was not just an effective meeting, but also an empowering experience for all participants. In time, my focus became how to enable family and friends to join together, feel connected, generate mutual support, and then plan and act together.

My vision is that we evolve a culture in which at least one in every five people feels confident and possesses the skills for family facilitation. These people will know how to create opportunities for families to gather for meetings, conversations, or celebrations, and how to guide these gatherings to increase group power and unity. Becoming such a facilitator does involve study and experience. To assist you on this path, this chapter begins with the basics of facilitation and then reviews more advanced practices for facilitating family councils. For this reason, consider this a resource chapter, one that you will return to periodically as you become a facilitator for your family and community.

Make Meetings Happen!

Family meetings, whether they involve just two people or the entire family, provide us opportunities to learn, teach, and co-power as we coordinate family life, resolve problems, plan important events, manage household chores, assist others, or explore opportunities. They also provide us another way to develop the practical communication and problem solving skills we need to be both effective family members and activists. Finally, family meetings serve as a powerful tool to create the culture of connection we desire, while inspiring us to act to heal and change the world.

Rebeca and I began setting aside time for meeting before we married. Sometimes it began with one asking the other whether we could talk about our relationship. At times the conversation occurred at that moment, and other times we would designate a time to talk about our expectations of each other and the prospect of developing a family together. Later, after having children, we initiated the tradition of planning meetings, which usually happened weekly, on Sunday mornings. The purpose of our meeting was to address such concerns as coordinating chores, negotiating understandings, resolving disputes, or planning activities. When other young people or adults came to live with us, they were integrated into our meetings. So we affirmed for ourselves what experts state, that regular family meetings are one of the best practices for healthy families.

All families can benefit from family meetings, whether it is single parents, stepfamilies, multigenerational families, or mixtures of family and friends. The meeting provides an arena for everyone to discuss problems and develop resolutions. When everyone, including the children, is fully involved, everyone feels ownership of the decisions. By working together as a family, the children come to recognize that groups can make good things happen. And adults too are reinspired by the intelligence and power of groups when there is mutual respect and connection.

Because of the hectic schedules that we live today, making time for meetings is a major challenge, so sometimes the best we can do is spontaneous, facilitated conversations. These are like the mini-meetings that occur during dinner or driving time, when you might ask everyone to help resolve a particular concern or to plan for an upcoming family activity. Still, the best strategy for supporting ongoing family development involves regular meetings. So I will first provide guidelines for effective family meetings, then give illustrations of their power for supporting family well-being and activism, and finally discuss some of the challenges involved.

GUIDELINES FOR EFFECTIVE

FAMILY MEETINGS

1. Be clear on the purpose.
2. Seek regularity.
3. Develop a group agenda.
4. Share with *conocimiento*, check-ins, or compliments.
5. Use facilitation.
6. Use brainstorming.
7. Make decisions by consensus.
8. Review and record agreements.
9. Plan family fun.
10. End with a positive closing.

1. **Be clear on the purpose.** Family meetings are to help members connect, support each other, solve problems, and plan. The meetings are not for parents or older siblings to lecture.
2. **Seek regularity.** Establish a regular time for meeting, maybe once a week, and make the meeting time a priority. Phones are unplugged and everyone commits attention to the meeting.
3. **Develop a group agenda.** Everyone is invited to contribute their issues or concerns to the agenda, including the young ones. If the list is long, prioritize items and carry over any that are not addressed for the next meeting.
4. **Share with *conocimiento*, check-ins, or compliments.** Start the meeting with everyone checking in with brief words about how they are doing, or by sharing a compliment or appreciation they would like to extend to others.
5. **Use facilitation.** The parent or chosen facilitator ensures that everyone gets to speak, the group stays focused on its agenda items, and that "put-downs" are not used.
6. **Use brainstorming.** To plan or solve problems, use the technique of brainstorming in which everyone is encouraged to freely contribute their ideas with no judgments made. Once the ideas are recorded, the group reviews the list to determine the best solutions.

7. **Make decisions by consensus.** Seek to find a decision that everyone can agree upon. Too often a majority vote creates divisions, so sometimes it is best to table a decision until the next meeting to give people more time to consider the resolution.

8. **Review and record agreements.** Toward the end of the meeting, review agreements to ensure that everyone's understanding is the same. Because we too often forget what we decided, someone should serve as recorder to document agreements and decisions. As soon as possible after the meeting, these can be posted on the refrigerator, or copies can be circulated to everyone.

9. **Plan family fun.** Incorporate into the meeting the planning of a family fun activity for the coming week.

10. **End with a positive closing.** Invite all members to share a final word. You can vary the request. For one meeting it can be a final feeling word, at another meeting a word about what you are grateful for, or an invitation to extend a compliment or appreciation to someone in the group.

Resolutions Sometimes Come from the Youngest

It is important for adults to remember that in a family meeting everyone has equal status in raising concerns and contributing to resolutions. Honoring this principle, we create experiences that co-power our young and often create better solutions. When our children were preschooler age, I brought a complaint to a meeting about the stress involved in getting the children dressed and then delivered to preschool in the morning. I was mostly looking for increased assistance from my wife, when our four-year-old, Andrea, made her observation and suggestion. She felt that I created a lot of "bad feelings" in the morning because I insisted on choosing the clothes she had to wear. If I would let her select her own outfit, she could dress herself, we wouldn't argue, and I could concentrate on dressing her little sister. Her observations were on point, and we only added to her suggestion that she select and lay out her clothes the evening prior. The immediate outcome was smoother mornings. The more developmental outcome was Andrea was owning her power for observation and problem solving.

Meetings Can Be Quick

After our meeting ritual was well established, most of our meetings became relatively short, except those requiring deeper discussions. Most participants brought their calendars and maybe a note pad. We would begin with a brief check-in, inviting each person to share "what's going on," usually something good and something challenging. Next, we developed our list of agenda items, including carry-over items from the last meeting and any new concerns. Agenda items could be proposed by anyone, and over time included every topic from resolving a sibling dispute or clarifying dating guidelines to planning for an upcoming family trip or determining how we could support a community project. The agenda items usually determined the length of the meeting, which typically required from thirty to forty-five minutes. Yet when someone was in a hurry, we usually found a way to end quicker and remain more focused on hearing and coordinating our schedules for the week. Finally, our closing was everyone sharing their final feeling word or phrase.

Meetings Can Be Used to Support Transformation

Our meeting tradition provided us a regular arena to explore ways of supporting family and community projects. Our Uncle Frank project illustrates.

On one occasion our daughters put on the agenda our upcoming trip to see Uncle Frank. Every couple of years we visited our uncle for a week. Despite essentially being a good person, Uncle Frank was exceedingly free in expressing his prejudice regarding immigrants, people of color, and gays. Our daughters wanted to discuss why we weren't confronting Uncle Frank on his racist comments. We explained our challenge in trying to be forthright in our beliefs and at the same time respectful to one of the family elders who was hosting us in his home. On this occasion we used our meeting to develop strategies to avoid conflicts with our uncle.

A couple of years later, before our next visit, the issue resurfaced, but this time we decided to be proactive and identify ways to address Uncle Frank's attitudes. Rather than avoiding him, our strategy became to engage with him, allow him to get to know us more deeply, and rather than argue with him, share our stories to illustrate the respect we have for African Americans, gays, and other people working for community betterment. Over the years, we have witnessed a significant change in Uncle Frank, to the degree that he is now a strong advocate and supporter of many of the people he used to demean. We realize that our interactions may not have been the most significant experience that changed his attitude, yet we know that we contributed. Our meeting discussion helped us better understand the meaning of respect and develop a team strategy to help change someone's prejudiced attitudes.

Meetings to Enlist Activist Support

Over the years, our family meetings helped to advance significant community projects. One of my visions when arriving in Castro Valley was to develop a neighborhood spirit on our street. Soon after moving in I suggested to Rebeca that we organize a street party to bring our neighbors together. Once I got several of the neighborhood kids and parents interested, I brought a request to our family meeting. I needed help to enthuse some of the other families to participate. Everyone did their part to make our first annual Eagle Street Fourth of July gathering happen. The event became so successful in bringing families together that it occurred regularly for twelve years, ultimately requiring minimal effort on our part.

Similarly, I tapped our family to support several other projects, including the initiation of an Earth Day celebration at our local elementary school, a local high school Latino leadership program, and what has become the annual Days of the Dead celebration at the Oakland Museum of California, which yearly involves more than 4,000 people in honoring our departed loved ones and celebrating Mexican-American culture. In going to our family meetings for support, I invariably received assistance, while our children were able to witness how community activities are initiated and developed.

The Challenging Meetings

Were all our meetings perfect, meaning everyone enthusiastically participated and the meetings ended with everyone feeling fulfilled? It wasn't for lack of trying, yet maybe 60 percent were satisfying to everyone and the others less so. While Rebeca and I tend to have favorable memories of our success, our adult children have different memories. Some of the identified shortcomings include not enough regularity, less than full commitment by everyone, unequal sharing of authority, and not enough monitoring of the talkers, or support for the nontalkers.

Being the parent and chief facilitator, I feel the greatest challenge was just getting everyone to the meeting. When the children were young, it was relatively easy because we had an organized schedule, including limited television. Later, when they were adolescents, it was more challenging because of everyone's competing schedules. In response, we would sometimes shift the meeting times, which invariably caused someone else some hardship. While I believed I served as an exceptionally fair facilitator, I now hear I was both too flexible in allowing some to dominate and too authoritative in focusing on my agenda items.

In retrospect, I feel the objective is not necessarily perfect meetings, but that families meet to converse, discuss, and plan. At the time, I felt many of our meetings were successful simply because we clarified a schedule and coordination plan for the week. And, periodically, we addressed significant items that made a difference for us and others. While our daughters have identified shortcomings in our meeting tradition, it has provided us all with lessons in communication, planning, and problem-solving that we have been able to use in our activist and professional work arenas.

Serving as a Family Facilitator

Our families, organizations, and work teams can all use caring people willing and able to serve as facilitators. So, in serving our families as facilitators, we also learn skills that will assist us in any of our other activist or work-related groups. How do we develop these skills? Commit, read, observe, improve your ability to communicate—and jump in and do it.

Those of us who have some position of authority in our families, like parents or older siblings, are at a tremendous advantage which we should optimize. We already have a recognized degree of responsibility and authority for caring for our family. Developing our facilitation skills will only make us more effective in our role. It also assists us in creating a family culture where there is more shared leadership and responsibility. So make the commitment to serve your family and develop your skills.

I am the oldest son in my family. While my brothers may have felt that the role came with a lot of privileges, I believe they now appreciate the significant responsibilities it also required. When I first took up the role of serving the family as a facilitator, it was not to grab for greater authority or control of others, but to create an environment where we could all communicate, be heard, and develop solutions to benefit the full group. This is the essential commitment of a facilitator, to create a space that welcomes and guides participation so that the group can address its concerns and advance the greater good. This is always easier said than done, so let's first review the practices of a good facilitator, and then some of the challenges.

In addition to the "Guidelines for Effective Family Meetings" presented earlier, a facilitator keeps in mind the following points:

- **Explain your role.** Beginning with the first meeting, ensure that everyone understands the facilitator's role, including yourself. Your purpose is to serve the group. Your responsibilities include guiding the meeting and supporting everyone's participation, and not manipulating the meeting for your own ends. Invite the group's feedback. "If during the meeting anyone feels I'm lacking in my responsibilities just say so, and I'll try to do better."

- **Value all voices.** Everyone has a voice, from the youngest to the oldest, and every voice counts. Always seek to invite and validate all voices to increase family unity, achieve better group results, and to develop the self-confidence and power of each individual.

- **Encourage respectful dialogue.** Respectful dialogue involves meaningful conversation in which all have the opportunity to talk and everyone is encouraged to actively listen. Help the group identify the theme or question that is important to them, and then coordinate the conversation as needed so that no one dominates and space is ensured for everyone to contribute. On occasion the talking stick (discussed in the next section) helps facilitate dialogue, particularly with the expression of feelings and encouragement of deep listening.

- **Nurture trust.** Just because we are related doesn't mean trust is assured. Trust must be nurtured by investing time to stay current and connected with each other. Use the meeting to provide the opportunity to share *conocimiento,* strengthen relationships, and nurture trust and unity.

- **Be sensitive to hear feelings.** Family meetings often create an opportunity for family to express feelings. Be sensitive to this when hearing participants' comments, because they may be wanting or struggling to express particular feelings. Such feelings often provide you and the family with tremendous insights into what really needs attention. You might ask, "What are you actually feeling about this idea?" Then be ready to acknowledge the feelings and respond to them. "John, I really hear that you feel excluded. How would you like us to follow up, or does the family have any ideas of how to respond?" By expressing and responding to feelings, the group often feels more connected and is better able to work together.

- **Plan and solve problems.** A major purpose of meetings is to effectively plan or solve problems. Be ready to use such tools as posing strategic questions, brainstorming, and recording on easel paper to assist the group to find solutions.

- **Use fun and humor.** Family gatherings should be pleasurable, so don't take your role so seriously that you squeeze out the joy. Ask for the family's help in keeping the meeting fun, and keep attention on both enjoying each other and getting the work done.

With these guidelines in mind, the best way to develop your facilitation skills is to use a mix of several learning strategies. Do more one-to-one *conocimiento* sessions with family members to get to know them better and to hear their expectations of you as facilitator. Read more about facilitation and observe meetings with a greater attention to what seems to work well or not work. And look for opportunities to facilitate more meetings to expand your experience.

This section started by urging parents and older siblings to step into the role of facilitating, yet the invitation goes out to any family member who feels the calling. You may have to do more homework, such as one-to-one *conocimiento* with your parents, elders, or older siblings, to secure authority and support. Yet, through each conversation they will learn to trust your intent, and you will build confidence and cooperation, until you are ready to begin.

Convening with the Talking Stick

Recently, Rebecca Victoria Rubi, a dear friend, single-parent mom, and highly regarded community activist, suddenly died of a massive stroke.[2] Following her memorial service, I asked family and friends to bless a talking stick that we could present to her five young adult children. The hope we shared was that this tool would assist them in their family meetings. After explaining the use of the talking stick to the youngest daughter, emphasizing how it often helps us become better listeners, she said that it was a great idea because every one of her older siblings are "great talkers."

In my indigenous tradition, the talking stick is used to facilitate family and community dialogue. When members gather to problem-solve or plan using the recognized staff, talking stick, or other symbolic item, this evokes a pact among all present. The person who holds the talking stick has the "word" or the authority to speak, and all others the commitment to active listening. The person holding the stick is responsible to share from their heart and speak their truth. When finished, he or she either sets the stick back down or passes it to the next person requesting to speak. Group members take turns speaking truth and listening deeply. For this reason, some have suggested that it be called the listening stick.

For many families, the talking stick serves as a powerful tool to enable active listening to each other's words, with deeper consideration of the other's message or feelings. Even though my nuclear and extended family had developed a fairly mature practice of respectful conversation, it wasn't until we introduced the talking stick that we were able to break out of our old patterns of anxiously waiting to speak, and to more deeply listen to and weigh others' words. Consequently, we introduced the option that anyone could request that we use the talking stick for serious dialogue. This occurred when one of our daughters wanted to ensure that we would hear her wants and respond thoughtfully to her request to renegotiate her teenage privileges. Aided by its use over the years, we have generally learned to be more courageous, honest, and respectful with our everyday communication as well. Yet, when we periodically bring out our talking stick for special occasions like anniversaries or our annual unity circles, it still feels inspiring to hold, and aids us all in sharing our heart words. Using the talking stick, families can maintain deep listening and respectful sharing without the use of a facilitator.

Whereas the talking stick is used in my cultural tradition, any family can use any object to symbolize the responsibility for honest speaking. What is essential is that everyone appreciates its significance. Donna brought her family together for their first organized family meeting and announced that she desired to begin a new chapter in their family life, one in which she made a stronger commitment to listen to others. She described the talking stick tradition, and offered a palm-size glass turtle that had been owned by her mother as their talking object. After a number of gatherings using the turtle, the family improved their communications and began having regular family meetings. The turtle was rewarded with a special place on the family mantle where it is available for special occasions. Similarly, another family adopted the use of a heart-shaped stone that one of the members found at the beach. What matters is introducing the talking object in a manner that assures the family appreciates its purpose to support respectful conversation.

Over the years, I have coached parents and teenagers in introducing the talking stick tradition to their families. My suggestion is to first approach one or two family members to get their support before bringing the idea to the full family. Through these initial conversations you develop support for the tradition and generate ideas for introducing it to the larger family. When it is time to introduce the idea to the full family, express your caring feelings for the family and your desire to use this tradition to improve communication. Explain that using the talking stick involves four simple principles:

USING THE TALKING STICK:

THE FOUR ESSENTIAL PRINCIPLES

1. Everyone's perspective is valued.
2. Speak honestly.
3. Be brief.
4. Listen attentively.

1. **Everyone's perspective is valued.** Everyone will have opportunity to share his or her words. The person holding the talking stick is the only one who speaks. There are no interruptions.
2. **Speak honestly.** The holder of the stick is responsible to speak from their heart and share their truth.
3. **Be brief.** Speak words that are important because they convey meaning or feeling. Don't speak merely to speak.
4. **Listen attentively.** Everyone in the circle is responsible to listen with an open heart and mind, concentrate on what is being said, and seek to understand.

If your family is like most, expect some degree of resistance. You might hear remarks like, "Who are you to say we have to meet this way?" "I can say my piece without having to hold a stick." "I personally don't care for any of this Indian or new age stuff." Be prepared to acknowledge their feelings and to gently persist with your request. "You are right, we don't need a stick to talk to each other, but many families have found it useful to slow down their conversations and to ensure that everyone gets heard, so again, I request we give it a try." You might consider who might challenge your request beforehand, and inquire about their concerns and enlist their support. Just giving this a little thought prepares you to be less defensive and

Using a talking stick helps facilitate thoughtful sharing and respectful listening.

more resourceful if the resistance occurs. And, whatever does occur, trust that you have done your best, and that good will come from your efforts, even when it is not immediately apparent.

Doing your homework in advance to generate support, a good introduction to the tradition, and, often, selecting the right occasion to begin, all help in enlisting family participation. While your vision may be using the talking stick to assist your family in dealing with conflict, it might be best to introduce its use first on occasions where the objective is simply positive sharing. Many families have had tremendous success using the talking stick for occasions like anniversaries, birthdays, Thanksgiving, or family reunions. On these festive occasions, you might give an introduction that sounds likes this: "We are all here to celebrate Dad's birthday, so to gift him with our well wishes, several of us propose we use a talking stick to share why we appreciate him. Whoever holds the stick is responsible to share their good heart words, and everyone else to listen. I would like to start and then I'll pass the stick." Introducing the talking stick tradition in this way makes it less threatening for many, and provides family members a reference experience so it can later be brought forward for other, sometimes more challenging, occasions.

For some families, the talking stick becomes a welcomed and honored tradition, inspiring them to share the practice with others. After being introduced to the tradition, Eduardo Salaz, director of diversity at Intuit, a major Silicon Valley company, invited me to train all the members of the company's diversity council on the use of the talking stick to facilitate "authentic dialogue" within company work groups. The feedback was so positive, not only regarding its use within the company teams, but within people's families, that I was invited to return and train diversity leaders on the principles of family activism, particularly doing *conocimiento*. Similarly, many teachers have integrated the talking stick tradition into their elementary school classrooms. In turn, there have been repeated occasions when students have asked if it would be possible to introduce the tradition to their own families. As a result, I and others who do parent education trainings more frequently include the family use of the talking stick in our programs.

Consider use of the talking stick tradition for those situations where your family or work team need to improve their skills for sharing and deeper listening, or to facilitate the expression of deep feelings without using a facilitator.

The Family Improvement Plan

Developing a family improvement plan can greatly assist your relatives in supporting each other and engaging in community service. When I taught community organizing, one of my course requirements was for students to organize a family meeting. Their assignment was to organize a council to develop a family improvement plan with three parts: (1) Design the council meeting and secure family support for it; (2) facilitate the meeting; and (3) document your family improvement plan. The initial resistance by students was understandable. Over two-thirds had never experienced anything close to a structured family meeting, or came from families or cultures where they felt they had no power or authority to initiate such a meeting. Also, some currently lived a considerable distance from their families. Together we found ways to overcome these challenges, and many dozens of students developed family improvement plans that tremendously influenced their own growth and the well-being of their families and friends. John's family meeting is a good example.

John was a young man who found this assignment daunting. He was the middle son of ten brothers and sisters, and was constantly ridiculed by his father and older siblings about the uselessness of his college education and his failure to contribute to the family's finances. Besides having minimal power within the family, he had a stuttering problem that worsened in front of even the smallest of groups. He visited me to present the impossibility of his project. My response was, "We just need to develop the right organizing strategy." As a result, he enlisted the support of his girlfriend, sister, and mother to plan and assist with the gathering.

The meeting was held to coincide with Mother's Day to optimize his mom's leverage to ensure full attendance. His mother extended the welcome and shared her request that everyone participate. While starting as one large group of eighteen, the family divided into three small groups to brainstorm their ideas about being a healthy family and to prioritize what they desired to improve. They later reconvened as the full family so each group could share their recommendations and make a plan.

The outcomes for the meeting exceeded all expectations. For the first time, father and older siblings expressed respectful regard for John, who had been the butt of jokes for years because of his academic inclinations. As part of the family improvement plan, the family decided to be more supportive of education and set up a scholarship fund to encourage the younger children to consider college. They also decided to continue having family meetings. Equally amazing, John's stuttering was dramatically reduced, and he began radiating a self-confidence that was noticed by many. Additionally, he and his girlfriend became more self-assured in their ability to be agents of change.

John's success can be attributed to various factors, including his commitment to the process, the enlistment of allies, and a clear strategy for producing the family improvement plan. The strategy is outlined in the following plan.

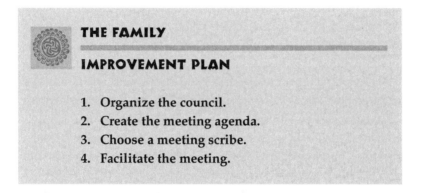

THE FAMILY

IMPROVEMENT PLAN

1. Organize the council.
2. Create the meeting agenda.
3. Choose a meeting scribe.
4. Facilitate the meeting.

1. Organize the council. Approach your family about organizing a council meeting to develop a plan for becoming a healthier family. Consider contacting each member one by one to develop buy-in and support. Approach your allies first to use their support to encourage the participation of others. Schedule a date and place that will allow for an uninterrupted one-and-a-half to two hour gathering.

2. Create the meeting agenda. The agenda typically includes the following:

- **Welcome and purpose.** Welcome the participants and review the purpose of the council—to connect as family and develop a family improvement plan.
- **Check-in.** Invite family to participate in a *conocimiento* exercise, with everyone briefly sharing something positive or challenging in their lives, or one of their positive traits.
- **Develop family vision and analysis.** Engage the family in several brainstorm exercises to develop the family's vision, with everyone responding on the following topics: (1) Ideally, how do we want our family to treat each other? (2) What are the best

positive qualities of our family? (3) What are the areas that need improvement?

- **Identify and prioritize family goals.** Review the brainstorm lists with the family to prioritize one or two goals that they would like to adopt, such as to treat each other fairly, to spend quality family time together, and so forth.
- **Develop a family improvement plan.** Identify several activities that will fulfill each goal. For example, for the goal of having more quality family time, the family might decide to share at least two dinner meals a week, to have regular family meetings, and to plan a family vacation. For each goal, assignments and starting dates should be identified.
- **Review agreements.** End with a review of agreements and assignments to ensure that everyone understands them.
- **Closing.** The closing includes an evaluation of the meeting. What did people like and what could be improved? Then everyone is invited to share a final feeling word.

3. **Choose a meeting scribe.** The meeting needs a note taker. During the meeting the family will brainstorm ideas and develop agreements. The best recording strategy is to hang several sheets of easel or butcher paper on the wall and use them to note the ideas generated by the group. This approach encourages participation and makes it easier to establish priorities. Either you or someone else may serve as the scribe. If the easel paper approach isn't possible, then someone can take notes on notebook paper. Because agreements and decisions are often established, it's important to document them and ideally review them before the meeting is completed. Later, it's important to provide the family a summary of their agreements.

4. **Facilitate the meeting.** Your role as the facilitator is to guide the family through the meeting process so that the sharing feels good, and the family improvement plan is developed.

While the main purpose of this assignment was to provide students with the experience of organizing a meeting and developing a

Taking notes helps everyone participate, follow the discussion, and review the decisions and agreements that are made.

family improvement plan, many students reported significant improvements in the daily life of their families. One family was finally able to discuss the unspeakable and with their mother developed a support plan for her final months of life. Another family discovered how they could pool resources to make their mother's dream of living closer to her family possible. A group of roommates not only developed a plan to maintain a more positive household, but also developed a strategy to help prevent one of their neighbors from dropping out of college. Most students guided their families to adopt regular meetings or at least to recognize them as a method they could employ when the need arose.

Whether your family is only you and your roommate or your larger circle, enlisting them to develop a family improvement plan can result in significant positive changes. The experience will also strengthen your ability to serve as a facilitator for other community groups or organizations seeking to develop plans for positive change.

The Family Council

There are times in our lives when major changes or significant events occur within our family that require what I call "special medicine," and that's what the family council is. While we often use family meetings to address day-to-day challenges, sometimes a more powerful meeting forum is required. This may be to organize extensive care for an ill family member, support family through a major life transition such as a divorce or death, to engage family and friends in a significant reunion or honoring ceremony, or to support a family healing. For the family council, the activist often needs to step up their commitment to do (or involve others in doing) the additional homework required to ensure that the council will serve the family well. I will provide several examples of councils and then some family council "best practices."

Councils Require Boldness and Homework

For the family activist, a key principle for successful family councils might be to "Just do it!" Three principles come to mind—be bold, do the homework, and use all your tools. In the first council I facilitated (discussed in Chapter 4), Rebeca and I had a clear purpose, to begin the process of *conocimiento* and healing that my family needed. Given the situation, it took boldness to initiate this first council and to do the homework required for a successful gathering, beginning with enlisting my father's support and then the one-to-one conversations with each family member to secure their commitment. The homework also included developing a proposed agenda that would help us connect and address the ailment our family was suffering, a combination of prejudice and ignorance surrounding gays, and the family's inability to handle difficult conversations. Finally, the homework required being prepared for whatever might surface at the meeting, with easel, paper, and pens ready.

I remember opening our gathering feeling determined and also insecure. Yet, once we started, my focus was on being fully present to listen, intuit, and facilitate. In the *conocimiento* session, when it became evident that we should shift direction to have everyone brainstorm the positive qualities they saw in each other, having the easel paper ready to document everyone's thoughts really helped. First, documenting the praises being offered was empowering because it validated each contributor, and, second, I saw how these documents would help to engage my absent brothers later on. Part of our follow-up homework was to share our experience with the brothers who had not attended and encourage their participation at the next family council.

Consider the Inclusion of Spirit

A similar, yet different level of commitment was required for another family council thirteen years later, when my father was suddenly afflicted with acute dementia as a result of what was supposed to be routine prostate surgery. Dad awoke after his surgery no longer remembering any of us, and the series of mini-strokes and violent flare-ups that followed initially made it unadvisable for him to return home, where he and our mother lived alone. Within a day our family reality became radically altered. Our family needed to immediately join together to make sense of our new situation, share emotional support, and formulate immediate and longer-term plans to support our parents.

Again there was the need to take the initiative to call for a family council, this time with a focus on requesting different family members to begin doing the homework required for an effective meeting. We all lived in different parts of the state, yet anticipating that my parents would need support, my request was that everyone begin evaluating their calendars and other realities and come to the council ready to determine how we might coordinate support. In addition, one brother was to research Medicare and insurance coverage, and our sister-in-law was to research the applicability of assisted living and acute care facilities. When we finally came together, our meeting was held in a way that would nurture and support us. We began with a prayer circle thanking Creator for our many blessings, asking for healing for our father, and guidance for all of us during this challenging time. During the council, there was time made to share feelings regarding the recent events, evaluate the latest information, listen, be heard, and plan.

While my brothers and I are not very religious, we are spiritual, and it only felt respectful of our parents to begin with prayer. We also felt that our father and family could use all the help available to assist us. So on this occasion we used prayer to invite the universal energy to work through us to aid and comfort our parents. While each of us have different ways of referencing this energy—God, Creator, the spirits of our ancestors, or simply the love that connects us—beginning with prayer helped us to become more spiritually present, reconnect, and commit to collaboration. Then we followed our agenda, and, considering everyone's realities, we developed short- and long-term plans to assist our parents.

Over the following weeks, then months, other meetings and telephone conferences were required, but based on the decisions made at our initial council, solutions to problems were always worked out. Our years of family meetings had also prepared us to be mutually supportive during difficult times. Given our prior experience, more of us were being proactive and doing the necessary homework to prepare for our family meetings. When we did meet, we all were contributing our best to make our council time effective and supportive. Our father died several months afterward, surrounded by much love and support.[3]

Maybe it was this experience with my father, or maybe it was just our time to understand, but we began to realize that powerful councils often incorporate sacred time and space in which we invite spirit, in the form of our loving essence or God, to be present. This can be done with prayer, creating an inspiration table or altar, taking time to breathe or meditate, or creating a cultural ceremony. Bringing everyone more in touch with their heart or spirit helps make the work and outcomes of family councils more harmonious, inspiring, and transformative.

Bringing the Family Together

Being clear about the potential and tools for facilitating family councils, we are more able to enlist the assistance of others and to innovate. The story of Lisa and her mother's pre-wedding gathering provides an excellent illustration.

From the time Lisa learned about family councils through our good friend Maria, she was looking for an opportunity to apply her evolving knowledge. It finally arrived when her mother announced to their family that she was marrying her companion, who also had adult children. Lisa, the twenty-four-year-old middle child of her family, saw the perfect opportunity to organize a family council. The purpose would be to bring everyone from the two families together to get to know each other better, envision how they wanted to relate to each other as this new family constellation, and to help plan the wedding. While she knew it was going to require homework, she was happy to organize the council as one of her gifts to her mother and new stepfather.

Assuming the role of the facilitator, Lisa reached out to several of her soon-to-be stepbrothers and sisters to begin planning. She discovered two of her prospective siblings had issues with their father, and at least one would not attend. Lisa remained positive and committed to moving forward with whomever attended. The invitation she sent out included an agenda and a request that each person bring a couple of items that symbolized what is uniquely special about themselves or their current family. As the family members arrived for their first council, they were invited to place their items on an inspiration table. To minimize distraction, Lisa had arranged for a friend to help care for several of the young grandchildren who would be present.

The agenda for the family gathering had three parts: get to know each other, hear the hopes and plans of the couple to wed, and to contribute ideas for a successful wedding event. During the first part of the gathering, each person introduced themselves by talking about the items they had brought. By sharing personal photos and mementos, the group came to know each other more deeply and set the context for hearing the vision of the two parents. The father's children expressed their regrets that two of their siblings had not attended, but were hopeful that good relations would develop over time. They took on the homework of informing their brother and sister of what transpired at the gathering, and reaffirming their welcome at the wedding. While there wasn't sufficient time for wedding planning, everyone felt it had been an inspiring and successful initial gathering.

When Your Best Efforts Don't Work

We can't always expect to have as successful a gathering as Lisa's. As activists we envision the best, follow through with the homework required, remain flexible given the dynamics that surface, and always remember that every conversation and meeting is only one step in an ongoing process to foster connection, unity, and positive family power. Yet, despite the needs and potential of our families, and our best efforts to organize meetings, sometimes our families don't or can't cooperate. The reasons can be many, from old patterns of childhood jealousies to serious hurts or addictions that need attention. Therefore, it's important to be hopeful, persistent, and flexible in our meeting objectives. Maybe just the process of trying to organize a meeting can begin the dialogue with family toward securing necessary professional assistance from a counselor, therapist, or minister.

Change, in families as in communities, takes persistence and time. Often, despite one's positive intentions, there is push-back from the family. As facilitators we need to accept that this is often part of the process. Maybe we need to devote more time to the homework or in the scheduling. Maybe we need more support, including possibly professional counseling. Maybe we need to evaluate or improve our communication skills, or to just continue moving forward with flexible persistence. The following are several examples of how facilitators responded to difficult experiences.

- Melinda secured everyone's commitment to participate in a family council after Thanksgiving dinner. She hadn't anticipated delays in preparing the dinner and the conflict with the televised football game. Before the council was to happen, her older brother rallied the guys to shift their commitment to the game, with the promise of doing the meeting later. It took all of Melinda's fortitude to manage her anger and hurt. The women decided to meet as a family women's council while the men watched the game. Given family issues they desired to address, they decided it was best to reschedule the council, yet to still hold a brief family circle after the game. After the game there were some brief apologies, and family members took a quick turn to share something they liked about the family and one way the family could improve. Upon Melinda's request, her cousin agreed to participate in a follow-up conversation between Melinda and her older brother. Despite the immediate disappointment, the process of building a more collaborative family had begun.

- Eric was looking forward to the council he had scheduled along with his wife for his three adult children and their partners, to request support for his evolving leadership role within their extended family. His youngest son arrived late and drunk, and began an altercation with his wife. Despite the drama, the family did share a conversation. While the meeting did not proceed as originally planned by Eric, the children developed agreements to support and hold their brother accountable for increasing his maturity and pursuing the treatment he needed. Gratitude was expressed to their father and stepmother for bringing them together, and a commitment was made to reschedule the family council. For a couple of weeks, Eric felt somewhat frustrated and depressed about the gathering and the challenges posed by his son. Finally, he reminded himself that taking care of your family is a lifelong commitment and that he had plenty of reasons to be grateful. Eric continues to be a father and grandfather who pursues the betterment of his family and community, recognizing that it is always a day-to-day challenge, and that by virtue of their fortitude, "we're winning."

- David, the fifty-year-old youngest adult son of his family, was facilitating a council for his extended family and felt that everything was going very well. Then at one point he gave his adult nephew-in-law some critical feedback. The nephew was offended. David got defensive, and before he could reground himself, his nephew gathered his family and left. David sought to minimize the situation and get the meeting back on track. The family regrouped and worked to end the gathering on a positive note, but David felt he had erred. A few weeks later, we spoke about the incident and determined that David had unintentionally disrespected his nephew in front of his kids, and to begin making amends would require David to apologize to his nephew. Given his commitment to the family, David plans to approach his nephew soon and begin the healing.

Best Practices

There are several good reasons to review best practices for family councils. First, considering these practices will make you more mindful of the preparation involved in organizing an ideal family council. Some of the preparations might require personal development goals, such as reaching out and doing *conocimiento* with family members, clarifying your own beliefs about spirit, or developing your communication skills. Second, the list can provide you and your allies with worthy ideas to consider as you plan for your family council. Third, you can apply these ideas to any of the activist or service organizations you work with, for the same strategies that support the health of our families can be employed to make our organizations more visionary, mutually supportive, and effective.[4]

Creating an inspiration table or altar invites spirit to be present at the family council.

The following are practices that contribute to successful councils. Remember that it is most important to design a gathering that works for *your* family, so innovate and do what will best support their needs. As you review the "Wisdom for Great Councils" practices, consider their application to both your family and at least one of the organizations with which you work.

WISDOM FOR

GREAT COUNCILS

- Reach out for input and support.
- Establish an inspiration center.
- Begin and/or end with sacred words.
- Incorporate *conocimiento*.
- Work from an agenda.
- Use easel paper to keep track of people's ideas.
- Record agreements and decisions.
- Be flexible.
- Share validations.
- Innovate.

- **Reach out for input and support.** You may have great intentions, yet unless there is support and input from your family you may not receive the commitment and participation desired. Call and meet with as many family members as possible to share your concerns and hear theirs. Follow up by providing members with an agenda in advance to clarify the meeting's purpose and time, such as "Saturday morning, 9 A.M. to 11 A.M., or until completed, followed by lunch."
- **Establish an inspiration center.** Establish a feeling of sacred time and place where the family can be inspired to be their best. Invite members to bring items reflecting the family's values or inspiration, such as photos of deceased parents and other ancestors. Before the gathering, set up a ritual center or inspi-

ration table where members can place their items, then, possibly at the beginning of the meeting, invite participants to share about what they brought. This ritual helps everyone feel the significance of the gathering.

- **Begin and/or end with sacred words.** Whether you call it prayer or sacred words, inviting love, spirit, or God's presence can establish a powerful positive tone for a council. One can invite an elder to extend an opening prayer, or everyone can be invited to share silence or a few words of gratitude. Later, ending with a prayer or words recognizing the contributions of all often validates the time that was shared and sets up a good feeling for future meetings.

- **Incorporate** *conocimiento*. Most powerful family councils are devoted to *conocimiento*, helping the family to get to know each other in a deeper way. You can begin the meeting with a short check-in in which members briefly share how they are feeling or what is current in their lives. This initial sharing brings everyone's voice to the council, informs the group about each person, and builds connection. Then the agenda may include or focus on doing *conocimiento* to enable greater mutual support, with questions such as, "What are your big goals or challenges this coming year?"

- **Work from an agenda.** Ideally, the facilitator has worked with others to formulate the initial agenda, which the full group reviews, refines, and approves. Given group agreement, the facilitator and group's responsibility is to stick to the agenda.

- **Use easel paper to keep track of people's ideas.** If there is going to be brainstorming and planning, tape easel or other large paper on the wall to record people's ideas. Making ideas visible helps generate group creativity and build agreements.

- **Record agreements and decisions.** Assign someone to take notes during the meeting. Agreements and decisions should be committed to writing and posted, or copies should be made for everyone.

- **Be flexible.** Many unanticipated issues can surface during family councils. It's best to be flexible and ready to change the agenda if necessary. An unexpected topic may emerge that the group feels is more important, or someone may think of a better way of addressing a specific problem. You may need to allow more time to resolve an issue, or it may even be necessary to schedule another meeting.

- **Share validations.** All of us thrive from genuine appreciation. Find ways for participants to validate the family as a whole or each other individually. Consider incorporating into the beginning or the ending the sharing of compliments in which each person expresses a brief appreciation for each of the other family members.

- **Innovate.** Be open and willing to innovate. Make the council work for your family or community.

PRAXIS

1. What experience or skills do you need to develop to serve as a good facilitator for your family? Who else among your family or friends could serve as a good facilitator? How might you collaborate to support each other's development?

2. What lessons did the discussion on the family improvement plan have for you? How might your family organize a council to develop your family improvement plan?

3. Plan your next family or group meeting in which you serve as the facilitator. Begin by preparing your action plan: What are your objectives? How will they serve the betterment of your full family? Who will be your support? What homework is required and when will it get done? Then organize the meeting and facilitate it. Afterward, celebrate and note your accomplishments and lessons.

11

FORMING UNITY CIRCLES

● ●

There is tremendous power when people gather in a circle. The circle serves to create a synergistic environment where people feel more connected and are better able to share and listen. In addition, many healing traditions recognize that the circle serves to facilitate healing by creating a vessel in which the positive energy generated by the group's sharing is enhanced, negative energy that participants may be carrying is dissipated, and the group's energy facilitates individual transformation.

My vision for society includes that, on any given day, thousands of circles of family and friends are expressing love for each other, gratitude for life, and optimism that we are making the world better for all. It involves people coming together as family and community, and sharing feelings and thoughts with each other that deepen connection, empower, and inspire. The best strategy for doing this is the unity circle. Learning to appreciate the power of these circles and how to facilitate them will prepare you with a valuable tool for making almost any group gathering an opportunity for inspiration. This chapter presents a series of examples of unity circles to activate your imagination around their many possible forms and to illustrate the role of the circle maker. The chapter ends with a review of key principles to assist the facilitator.

What Is a Unity Circle?

Unity circles are most often informal ceremonies that we can create within any family or community gathering to invite participants to

181

share heartfelt words honoring the person or occasion being recognized. They are most often joyful, spiritual, and inspiring, and serve to develop greater connection and unity among participants. They also provide an ideal opportunity to inspire participants to commit or recommit to their own growth or to serving the community. The unity circle I facilitated for Blas Guerrero and his family begins to illustrate the remarkable power of this simple ritual.

I arrived a little late to my friend's graduation party. Blas was the first in his family to graduate with a doctorate degree, and he had invited family from the entire Southwest to his home to celebrate. Many were there, and everyone was enjoying the beautiful day, the food, the music, and good companionship.

After a half hour of mingling, I noticed that while family and friends were very proud of Blas, no special recognition had been shared or appeared to be planned for the occasion. I knew the celebration could blossom with a unity circle, so I searched for our host. When I found Blas, I asked him if he would like me to lead a unity circle. He was honored, so I suggested that we spread out and let people know that in fifteen minutes we were initiating an honoring circle in the backyard.

At the appointed time, we turned off the music while a couple of people circulated around the house inviting everyone to step outside. Once the circle was formed, I introduced myself and welcomed everyone on behalf of Blas and his family. I acknowledged that many here were feeling pride in Blas's achievement, and underscored the importance of sharing our feelings and thoughts with each other on this occasion. I then invited everyone to introduce him or herself, state how they knew Blas, and offer any short words they had for him or the *familia*. To assist us in sharing, I offered the use of the talking stick I had brought for this special occasion, reminding everyone that whoever held the stick had the privilege to speak and everyone else the responsibility to listen.

The sharing that followed was inspiring for everyone. We heard from young and old—words of love, pride, hope, and happiness. After about twenty minutes of words from family and community, I asked Blas to step forward and receive the talking stick just blessed

Unity circles transform ordinary occasions, such as this housewarming, into meaningful and transformative experiences.

by the group's sharing and to speak his words. He expressed his gratitude, his story of struggle, and his commitment to continue doing his part to ensure success for all young people. As we all looked at each other, we saw inspiration radiating from our teary eyes, tears of pride and hope.[1] We ended with several rounds of applause done in the style of the United Farm Workers tradition and then hugs.[2]

Too often we join together as family and friends without creating the opportunity that could really connect and inspire us with the joy of being together. When we gather for a graduation, a birthday dinner, or another special occasion, this inspiration can be achieved by introducing a unity circle. We can transform an ordinary gathering into a shared experience that moves people to feel their spirit and connection, and strengthens our commitment to increase love in the world.

Serve as a Circle Maker

Whether it is a family or community gathering, unity circles serve to nurture connection among family, friends, and others, bringing tremendous energy, power, and hope. Our families and communities could become a greater force for positive change were there more people available to serve as circle makers among us. The circle maker is like a specialized facilitator, one who is dedicated to bringing people together for the expression of heart words. The following unity circle examples illustrate the many opportunities available for circle making, and the role of the facilitator or circle maker.

Many people initially view unity circles as a contrived family or community ritual, then with experience they come to respect the tradition as medicine for nurturing connection and love. It may appear that people are being brought together to merely share words to honor a person or an occasion, yet as facilitators we are doing much more. We are forming a space of safety and respect, and inviting people to participate in an opportunity to express love and feel unity. We are serving as circle makers.

Sharing within circles is always powerful. Consider your own experience of sitting with others in an informal circle sharing a meal, dialogue, or work. The experience of being in a circle and exchanging conversation fosters feelings of connection and group spirit. Add the intention of sharing caring words and magic occurs. This is circle making—bringing people together to create a purposeful environment for exchanging meaningful feelings and thoughts. In this environment, members express respect, relationships deepen, and unity among participants evolves.

Most of our families already join together for special occasions, such as an anniversary, a birthday, Thanksgiving, or maybe Mother's Day. Our role is to assist the group to optimize the connection and inspiration that can occur on such occasions by joining people together to share positive words. After doing the preliminary homework to ensure support for the circle, when the time comes you draw people together, provide a welcome, and facilitate introductions. You might begin by saying something like this: "We are here today to honor Mom for Mother's Day. So we are each going to take a turn to share with Mom why she is special to you or offer a short 'Mom story' that illustrates this. Afterward, Mom can share her own thoughts." As the circle maker, you provide leadership to bring the group together and to set forth a context for inviting everyone to share.

For many families or groups of friends, the initial unity circle takes a little preorganizing because people are not accustomed to the practice. It's important to speak to the person being honored and at least a couple of others to ensure a "critical mass" of people who will actively support and share when the circle is called. It is also helpful to use several other "medicines" to help create the environment for a positive circle. Some of these are: an opening prayer, a talking stick, an inspiration table, and the traditional unity circle design described below. Mark's birthday party illustrates the role of the facilitator, the use of the talking stick, and the powerful outcomes that can occur through the unity circle.

Mark invited a full house of family and friends for his thirtieth birthday party and asked me to facilitate a unity circle. As the time neared for the birthday cake, I called for people's attention and announced that it was time for the unity circle to honor Mark's birthday. I explained that on occasions of birthdays we use the unity circle to celebrate and honor the birth of our dear friends by sharing how they have been a gift to us and to extend our well wishes for them. I also explained that we were going to use the talking stick to facilitate our speaking from the heart.

We arranged ourselves in a circle—actually it was a large oval— and I started by briefly sharing how Mark and his commitment to support our youth have repeatedly inspired me. I passed the talking stick, and in this way family and friends took turns sharing their appreciation for Mark. Repeatedly we were touched by the love expressed. Several of his family shared the pride they felt hearing about Mark's community service and now experiencing the community he had developed around him.

As is often the case, the youngsters were also touched by the love and felt the courage to share. At one point, six-year-old Diego García, the son of Mark's landlord, requested the stick. He thanked Mark for being his friend and expressed his hope to be like him when he grew up. Hearing this youngster articulate so clearly his feelings and vision left many of us feeling hopeful, and we were also touched by the love and courage we witnessed in the circle that afternoon.

Sensing a completion in the sharing, I requested the talking stick, presented it to Mark as our collective gift to him, and invited him to share his words with us. Mark, who was clearly emotionally moved, expressed his gratitude for having all of us as family, for the words we shared, and for the present moment in which his community of family and friends had become one. His birthday wish was that everyone present would continue doing their part to ensure justice for our community and to be community with each other.

Before we had eaten a single piece of cake we were all feeling energized with love and hope. Later Mark shared with me that he had never experienced such appreciation, and that for the first time he felt his family really knew what he was about. In the interactions that continued that evening, it was evident that many had learned the power of the unity circle.

The caring spirit and activist commitment that we aspire to nurture among our family and community are never the result of one experience, but grow through many experiences we create that validate, teach, and inspire. We organize the unity circle for the immediate outcome of group expression and inspiration. Yet, we also look forward to the additional outcomes that will result, such as enhanced connection, group unity, or social responsibility.

Do you remember little Diego who was inspired to speak at Mark's party? Almost eight years later, I had the opportunity to talk with him. At fourteen years old, he is working as a counselor at a leadership development camp for urban youth. For him the greatest takeaways from his unity circle experiences are his feelings of personal power, his connection to spirit, and his positive sense of community. "Every time I am part of a circle, I feel connected with everyone else and feel that my life has real purpose, to make our community better for everyone." While he plans to be an engineer, he knows that his life will be about "giving back to the community."

cance of the occasion—to share love, extend honor, and celebrate. If there are new people present, a short explanation is provided to ensure their comfort and enable their participation. As the facilitator, you might invite the host(s) to extend the welcome.

Opening prayer and/or introductions. In many cultures, significant family or community gatherings begin with a prayer or another form of ritual to help participants be fully present with mind and spirit. Whether it is a prayer to God or the spirits of our ancestors, or an invitation for all to be present in love, I find opening in this way makes for much more powerful unity circles. It makes the time feel extra special and sacred. Many of the participants will reach further within themselves to connect with their spirit, and in so doing they create a group energy that is more inviting of love. The prayer can be quite short: "Creator, thank you for this beautiful day and that we could all join together. Through our sharing today, may we leave inspired to extend greater love in the world."

A different or supplemental approach is to invite everyone to briefly introduce themselves, their relationship to the honoree, and why they are present. This is especially appropriate when the group includes many people who do not know each other or have not seen each other recently. The introductions bring everyone's energy to the circle via their voice and helps connect the group.

In my indigenous tradition, we often incorporate a sage-burning ceremony in the opening. At the outset of a gathering, we light the dry white sage leaves and fan them to burn and create smoke as we begin our prayer. For us, the smoke represents the Creator's breath and signifies the beginning of sacred time and an invitation for all to be fully present in body and spirit. While I believe that integrating prayer into unity circles multiplies the love or spirit power of the group many times over, your responsibility as a circle maker for your group is to conduct the opening in a manner that respects the immediate opportunity and those present.

The Traditional Unity Circle Design

Almost any circle organized with positive intent can en
feeling for those being honored and for the participants.
of the traditional unity circle design aids the family and
optimize the opportunity to connect, inspire, and gener
energy for change as well. The traditional unity circle de:
marized below and then explained.

UNITY CIRCLE

DESIGN

1. Form the circle.
2. Welcome.
3. Opening prayer and/or introductions.
4. Invitation for heart words.
5. Closing.
6. Invitation for hugs.

1. **Form the circle.** The well-formed circle is powerful medi
   circle serves as a container to hold and create energy, an
   the beginning of sacred time. People come to the circle as
   beings, each carrying their own thoughts and emotions.
   ing in the circle connects the individuals into a network o
   or community energy. As facilitator, you can open the ce
   by calling the circle together with a verbal announcemen
   using a spoon to clink on a glass. In my Chicano tradition,
   a drum and a particular drumbeat that signifies that it is ti
   the community to join together.

2. **Welcome.** The welcome is essential to mark the beginning
   unity circle and helps ground people regarding the purpose
   event. The welcome invites all to be fully present to the si

4. **Invitation for heart words.** The unity circle is organized for sharing heart words particular to the specific occasion, whether it be
to honor a person or to express sympathetic words or good
wishes. Your responsibility is to invite these words so as to
encourage participants to speak from a place of emotional truth
that honors the honoree, themselves, and the other participants.
This can be done by providing a clear invitation that incorporates
a strategic question and then by modeling.

In the request, you reiterate the purpose of the event and provide a clear "invitation question" and instructions. The invitation
question informs the group how to participate. The following
example illustrates: "Family and friends, we are here to celebrate
the twenty-year anniversary of Sergio and Amelia. As our gift to
them, I invite you to share how their union is special to us, and
any blessing words you have for them. I'd like to start, and then
we can go around the circle to the left, and everyone who would
like can take a turn to share their words." It would then be effective to take a short pause before proceeding. "Sergio and Amelia,
thank you for loving each other and creating a family that inspires
me to be more committed to advancing love in our world. I wish
you continuous health and love." Through the instructions and
the modeling, participants receive a clear understanding of how
they might honor our friends. For larger gatherings, a talking
stick is useful for facilitating the sharing.

After the group has completed their sharing, you invite the hon-
oree(s) to speak. Knowing the power of this opportunity, you
should inform, and maybe even coach, the honoree beforehand
about speaking. As a family activist, you recognize this is an important moment for family and friends to hear a statement that affirms
their love and challenges them to be and do more as a family or
community. For this reason, you ensure that the honoree knows
that they will have a time to speak and that they might want to use
this opportunity to say what is truly in their hearts.

5. **Closing.** After all the heartfelt expression, you want to end the
unity circle in a way that encourages the group to continue living

the positive feelings that have been shared. The closing ideally affirms the unity, love, and commitments that were shared. Various ways to close include a request for final feeling words, a call for commitments, the holding of hands, a final prayer, or a combination of all. As every unity circle experience is different, your role as the facilitator is to stay aware of the group's energy, and transition to a closing when the time is appropriate. This may be when you feel that all who desire to speak have spoken or, if time is limited, that sufficient thoughts and feelings have been shared to reflect the positive sentiments of the group. At that time, you might suggest that the group close by standing and holding hands, and then you might ask for each person to share a final word expressing their heartfelt feelings. The group will typically express words like "love," "connected," "proud," or "family" that will serve to reaffirm their positive experience. Or you might request a commitment. "Given what we heard about our Uncle

A family unity circle for the Days of the Dead.

Art, what commitments do we each wish to make to our family or community, in a single word or phrase?"

Finally, you can offer a concluding reflection or prayer that affirms the entire experience. For example: "Creator, again we give thanks for the opportunity to honor our dear friend and express our love. We ask that you continue assisting us all to be the force of good needed in our world."

6. **Invitation for hugs.** Hugs are amazing. Once you get comfortable with them, they express and teach love. In our society we are not provided enough opportunities to connect emotionally, spiritually, or physically. For this reason, at the closing of the unity circle, put forth the request that the circle end with each person extending a hug to at least three others. The hugs make the emotional experience of sharing feel real and in turn often work their own magic. Family members and friends often reaffirm their wish to stay in touch, and conversation dates are established to continue the connection. Exchanging hugs has led many groups to begin a major shift in their family culture. They hug more!

Principles to Guide the Circle Maker

Through the prior examples I have sought to illustrate the responsibilities of the circle maker. The circle maker offers or is invited by family and friends to facilitate a unity circle. Whether the group is three people or a community group of dozens, your role is to make it easy for participants to join together and express from the heart. The following principles add more specifics to your role in applying the traditional unity circle design:

1. **Serve as the circle maker or facilitator.** Circle makers can never create the circle alone. We need the active support of others, yet we do need to recognize our responsibility. We invite participants to form a circle, provide guidance, facilitate sharing, and ensure a closing. To prepare yourself, a brief meditation or prayer is useful for reconnecting with your spirit. What is your purpose? Is it to

facilitate connection, inspiration, and love? And what else? I always offer a prayer thanking Creator and asking that I be used as a force for advancing love and respect.

2. **Inform a core group of the plan.** However informal or formal the anticipated plan for the unity circle is, have a plan and a few people willing to help. Prior to or on the occasion, inform the supporters of the plan and make clear your request for their assistance. Usually they help organize the group, enlist group cooperation, and then model positive sharing.

3. **Create the environment.** Call people to the circle verbally or by use of a drum, rattle, or other instrument. As stated earlier, there is incredible power in the circle arrangement. Participants feel more included and connected, plus it helps to focus the group's energy and attention. To the degree possible, seek to create a circle where everyone can be seen and heard.

4. **Provide a welcome, expectations, and invitation questions.** A brief opening includes words of welcome, a simple statement of why we have gathered, explanation of the intention of the circle, and brief instructions regarding the sharing. The intent of this opening is to inform the group about the purpose of the unity circle and to prepare them for participation. The introduction might also include a brief mention of your role: "My name is Rebeca, and I am here to facilitate this unity circle to honor our dear friend." As explained earlier in the description of the unity circle design, clear "invitation questions" are essential to assist people to participate. Develop these questions in advance. As simple as these questions may appear, they often require several iterations before they carry the clarity you desire.

5. **Maintain the respect and focus.** Many people are not accustomed to sharing in respectful ways. Initially feeling uncomfortable, they may even create distractions for others by giggling, joking, interrupting, or withdrawing. For this reason the facilitator reminds participants of the intention and the need to balance

our feelings of joy and respect during the ceremony. The use or presence of alcohol is discouraged before or within the circle.

6. **Draw upon your intuition and spirit.** Even as you are doing your best as a facilitator, unexpected group dynamics will often surface that require attention. Don't panic—trust your good intentions, intuition, and spirit. If old hurts or angers surface, acknowledge the feelings and assure the person concerned that they will be addressed later, possibly with the aid of the group. That such challenges can arise is one reason why I prepare myself with a request for the Creator's guidance, so that I feel there will be intuitive wisdom available to me. Also, it's important to know that we don't have to be perfect, just responsive and responsible.

7. **Ensure a closing.** A good circle ends with a clear closing. Whether it is a thank you, applause, a statement of transition, a final prayer, or a one-word sharing—followed by hugs—a closing is essential.

Utilize these principles in combination with your good intention and intuition, and you will experience circles that are amazing. There will be expressions of courage, love, and respect that will touch and inspire all gathered. Participants will feel connected and motivated to be more loving. As you recognize the significance of your role, remember to learn from every experience. Each facilitation prepares you for the next and strengthens your capacity to help your family, friends, and community to thrive.

Honoring the Dead to Inspire Our Activism

Family activists are continually looking for opportunities to help our families and communities grow in their commitment to support each other and community transformation. Memorial services for those who have died are special occasions where we have the opportunity to support family bereavement and healing, honor the deceased loved one, and foster the commitment of those gathering to live more fully the love and transformation we desire in the world.

The following story of María's memorial service illustrates what we can do as circle makers to serve our family and communities.

One of the most life-changing events is the death of a loved one. During this time of loss, as difficult as it can be, we are also given the opportunity to evaluate the meaning of life and the significance of our own lives. Are we living life fully? Are we making the contribution we are here to make? In remembrance of a loved one who died, how will we live better lives?

The memorial service for a loved one has the potential to be transformative in our life and the lives of others. The service can convey the story of our loved ones in a way that honors them, supports the healing of those present, and inspires us to become better people, or it can be a dull ritual that neither heals nor inspires. When I was a young man, I experienced a service of the latter type that I related in the introduction to this book, which made me vow to become an advocate for ceremonies that truly honor the dead and inspire us to adopt or continue the positive values or practices of our departed loved ones. I decided to learn how to facilitate memorial services that inspire love and transformation.

By the time our community heroine and dear friend María Vargas suddenly died, I was experienced in facilitating numerous forms of unity circles.[3] When friends and family met to determine how to best honor her, I offered to facilitate our meeting to plan María's memorial service. Initially the meeting was tense because each of us knew María from different networks or communities and had different perspectives on how to proceed. But soon we recognized how special she had made each of us feel, and realized the challenges and lessons she was leaving us—to learn how to honor our diversity and exchange love with each of our encounters. With this clarity, we planned the service to incorporate the various spiritual and musical traditions that she loved, and to create the opportunity for the many varied people she called family and friends to become community with each other. The group asked me to facilitate the service.

A couple of days later, more than 500 people attended María's funeral service. Most were still coping with the shock that our wonderful friend had so unexpectedly died. Teacher, mentor, therapist, role model, and advocate for youth, women, and justice, she meant so much to us that we struggled to conceive of life without her. However, we were present to honor her, and how better than by connecting as community, recognizing her best qualities, and dedicating ourselves to integrating those values and commitments into our own lives.

The first step was to bring people together. I opened the service by asking everyone to turn to a neighbor, introduce him- or herself, and express to each other the gifts María had given them or us. Afterward, I invited the group to give voice to those gifts. We heard each other say: "love," "hope," "courage," "inspiration," "love of music," "made me feel special," "a role model," "she healed my family and me," "how to be a strong woman," "how to enjoy being single," "remember your roots," and so forth. Then I asked, "What values will we continue taking into the world in her memory?" As I heard each commitment, I repeated it: "to love each other," "to love life," "to battle for the youth," "to think critically," "to be a voice for justice," "to continue the struggle," "to take care of myself," "to jog," "to create community everywhere I go," "to be an excellent therapist," "to support my daughter through college," "to listen to her voice because she's still with us."

Ten years later, many of us who participated at her service still encounter each other in a grocery story or at a community protest and remember our bond to María's life and our dedication to continue living her values. Even if we did not know each other before, we now share the love we experienced through María at her funeral. Many of us continue to place her photo on our altars as a reminder of our commitments, and of her presence as a spirit that continues to promote love, family, and justice.

As circle makers, our vision is to attend to our family and friends in ways that nurture love and inspire us to serve each other and our community. In so doing, we develop more confidence to be loving to others. We can use the medicine of unity circles to facilitate the inspiration and community building that make us a force for cultural and social change.

PRAXIS

1. Have you ever experienced a unity circle or something similar? What made it meaningful for you? How did it benefit you, those participating, or the larger movement for social transformation? Having read this chapter, can you imagine being a circle maker? What might it take to prepare yourself for facilitating a unity circle?

2. Next time you go to a party or celebration of family or friends, notice what happens or doesn't happen to bring people together to share meaningful group expression. In light of your knowledge of unity circles, what do you see could have happened? How might it have been organized? Imagine that you had facilitated a group circle that led to meaningful sharing and inspiration, then list in bullet notes what you did, how you were supported, and how people participated in a positive way. Doing this numerous times has prepared me with many potential plans so that when the opportunity to facilitate a circle arises, I can draw on both my actual and imagined experience.

3. Determine when you might facilitate your first or next unity circle. Develop your plan and build your support. Facilitate the circle. Whatever happens, remember to honor yourself and those who contributed for the gift you offered to others. Afterward, note your lessons. What did you learn about groups and facilitation that will help you with your next circle?

PART III
MOVING FROM FAMILY
TO COMMUNITY POWER

The creative potential of the world's hundreds of millions of
Cultural and Spiritual Creatives is being expressed through the
formation of communities of convergence in which people
develop relationships, institutions, and authentic cultures of
living societies. A community of convergence may be as
simple as a local study group. It might be a farmers' market, a
school to develop inquiring minds, or a course on voluntary
simplicity. It might be a socially responsible local business,
a church congregation devoted to spiritual inquiry and
community service, or a holistic health clinic. No matter how
small or isolated such initiatives may originally be, each
creates a protected space in which diversity, experimentation,
and learning can flourish to create the building blocks of a
new mainstream economy, politics, and culture.

— DAVID C. KORTEN, THE GREAT TURNING[1]

12

CREATING POWERFUL FAMILY AND COMMUNITY GATHERINGS

A primary intention for this book is to provide tools for empowering our families and friends to serve our larger community as love in action, by committing to being family with each other while engaging in cultural and social change. Now that we have reviewed the essential tools of the *Familia* Approach for connecting, co-powering, facilitating family meetings, and creating experiences that inspire, I offer here several examples of how these tools can be used to support powerful family or community gatherings that aid us in becoming beloved community.

Creating Family

We repeatedly hear the adage that it takes a village to raise a child. This may work for many villages because all members feel responsible for the children in their community; that is the expectation that they hold for themselves and each other. How can we generate a similar feeling among family and friends today? One way is by developing the pact of being family with those we wish to be close with. The following example illustrates the tradition we are evolving to recognize and celebrate the commitment of becoming family in a way that nurtures increased community connectedness. While the strategy is grounded in our Chicano culture, it could be easily adapted to resonate with many other traditions.

Within our community, we have evolved formal and informal traditions for adopting and creating family. Often our relationship with close friends becomes so family-like that we use the first opportunity that surfaces to make them our *compadres* or *comadres*, which literally means coparents, or in popular usage, "dear friends." When we initially present our children to the community, or for their baptism, *quinceañera* (a traditional coming-of-age celebration for young girls on their fifteenth birthday), or wedding, we often select a close couple to serve as their godparents. Already treated like an adopted brother, sister, cousin, or best friend, they become official *compadres*, coparents to our children, or at least important friends to us and them.

The first time I was made a *compadre* and godparent I felt greatly honored, and took my role seriously. In my early organizing years, I lived away from home and on an austere budget, so I felt blessed that the Soto family considered me enough like family to always have a chair for me at their dinner table, even when they were straining to make ends meet. When it came time to baptize their son, they asked me to be the godparent. I wanted to fulfill this responsibility well, so we made explicit their expectations of me and my commitment as godparent to their son. For the next fifteen years that we lived relatively near to each other, we were readily available to each other for child care, to support each other's organizing projects, or to share family time. Thirty years have passed, and I remain a committed and supportive friend to my godson.

As others in our extended network chose to formally make their friends their family, I was often called to facilitate a ceremony or unity circle. My requirement for facilitating the ceremony was that the family and godparents met first and articulated mutual expectations. If it was going to be a baptism ceremony, they had to clarify the expectations and commitments of the godparent to the child. If the occasion was to be a *quinceañera*, the young person would have to meet with her new godparents to clarify mutual expectations. Subsequently, I would meet with them to design the ceremony making public to family and friends their commitments to each other.

Lorena García's presentation ceremony illustrates how commitments are made public and friends come to recognize each other as family. Lorena's dad, Lorenzo, contacted me to share his frustration and vision. He was no longer a practicing Catholic, yet he wanted his daughter to benefit from having godparents in her life. Ideally, he wanted to formally adopt several godparents for his daughter, including my wife and me, his brother, and his former sister-in-law, Loraine. He asked for my assistance to design and facilitate the ceremony. As Lorena was twelve years old, we decided to call it a presentation ceremony because we were presenting her to the community as a preteenager. We scheduled a meeting with the selected godparents. At our meeting, I asked Lorena what her expectations were of her new godparents, and in turn asked the godparents about their expectations and commitments.

On our ceremony day, family and friends gathered at the Fire Circle picnic area in the Oakland hills, overlooking the Bay Area. We prepared the grounds for the unity circle by placing stakes at each of the cardinal points and blessing the circle with the burning of sage. Then we came together and the unity circle began with the welcome and prayer salutations to each of the directions. During these prayers, an eagle appeared over the circle, which we saw as a good omen. We then proceeded with the ceremony.

I asked Lorena's parents to state the purpose of the gathering and to present Lorena by sharing with our community the personality they saw evolving in their daughter. Afterward, I asked Lorena to introduce her godparents and say why she had selected them. Inviting the new godparents into the circle, I asked each to share the commitments they were making to Lorena and her family. Loraine shared her promise to always be there as a friend, an aunt, and a godparent. Lorena's uncle committed himself to always be available, to learn from her, and, hopefully, to impart some of his experience. Rebeca and I expressed our commitment to support her in our prayers and in learning about our culture and our tradition of giving back to the community.

As a token of our collective commitment, we asked the group to assist us in blessing a gift necklace for Lorena. As the necklace was passed around the circle, everyone was invited to extend their blessings to Lorena by holding it and sharing their words. After everyone spoke, the necklace was presented to our new goddaughter, who was then invited to speak. Lorena was thanking everyone for their good wishes when a deer came down near to the circle and just stood there, seeming to be listening to her words. Lorena acknowledged all in the circle as family and also promised to do her best to become a person who would make us all proud. To close, I asked everyone in the group to express in a word or phrase what they felt from this circle. People exclaimed, "love," "respect," "hope," and "pride." Then I asked, "What will we take from this circle to share with our own families?" This time we heard, "love," "respect for our young people," "commitment to communication," and "a commitment to fight for a healthy world for our children's children." We finally ended the circle with an invitation for all to share hugs.[1]

Eighteen years later, there are significant individual, family, and community outcomes to note. Lorena graduated from the university with advanced degrees and works as the director of fund development for a legal advocacy center. Her godmother, Loraine, continues to be her friend, counselor, and aunt, and her uncle Pablo has fulfilled his intentions to provide support and encouragement. Rebeca and I are always glad to see Lorena when we can. She credits much of who she is today to her father, who always ensured that she was surrounded by family and friends committed to community and family activism.

Many of us who participated in the ceremony felt that it affirmed that we were part of the extended García *familia* or beloved community. Consequently, when Lorenzo, Lorena's dad, launched a citizen's education and voter registration organization, *Votantes Unidos* (United Voters)[2] and came to us for support, many of us who were part of his beloved community extended our financial or volunteer support because on the occasion of this unity circle, and others that we shared, we had made or affirmed commitments to be *familia* and fight for a healthier community.

Unity Circles Create Miracles

What are miracles? When a young person discovers he is truly loved and respected by others, is that a miracle? Is it a miracle when a family learns how to listen and communicate with each other? I believe that any personal or group growth that helps us become better people can be seen as a miracle. These are miracles because they represent an evolution in our ability to be more human, an evolution that may not have happened without some extraordinary event to catalyze or support this growth.

Unity circles can make miracles happen. As a facilitator, you plan and guide a circle to nurture unity, inspiration, and happiness, and then you expect the unexpected. Knowing that miracles can happen makes us more sensitive and creative in our role. The following story is about applying the *Familia* Approach to support the development of our young people and about the multiple transformations that occurred.

I am a godparent to the Castro family, and for years I served as a facilitator for their family ceremonies, including birthdays, baptisms, and *quinceañeras*. Many of these gatherings included a number of young men who were friends of their young adult sons, some of whom were street tough and somewhat reserved during the ceremonies. While not participating directly, these young men were usually present as active observers. Several times after an event, a couple would approach me to ask if I would do a circle "just for the guys." I would tell them, "Call me when you're ready," and they finally did.

One of the young men, Rick, asked if I would help him organize a ceremony for Tomás, who was leaving in a few days for the navy. Their group of six guys had been partners throughout high school, and while most objected to Tomás going into the navy, they respected his decision and wanted to send him off in a good way. They wanted the ceremony to occur outdoors with a campfire.

On a Friday night, we drove into the hills to a local campground. David, Rick's older brother, joined us for this gathering. We found an isolated area, and soon we were sitting under a canopy of pine trees around a warming fire, the flames flickering against the dark night. When one of the guys pulled out his liquor bottle, I reminded them that alcohol and smoking were not appropriate during ceremony time.

We formed the circle and I invited Rick to extend the welcome, then I asked the group to stand while I explained why we burn sage: "We burn white sage to create sacred time and to invite our courage, our spirit, our elders, and other loved ones to be with us." I lit the sage, extended prayers to each of the directions, and then walked around the circle smudging each person with the sage smoke.

To begin, I asked them to share names of people or ancestors they wanted to invite to our circle that night. The names of grandparents and friends were shared, and then one name was mentioned that touched several of the young men. Antonio García had been killed the previous week. He was one of our community heroes, a good and caring person who had been shot dead by a young woman high on drugs. In remembrance, he was brought into the circle.

A little later, I asked the young men why they had come to the circle. David immediately spoke. "I know this isn't my crew. I met you through my lil' bro, but you're all partners with my bro so that makes us *carnales* (brothers).[3] So I hope it's cool that I'm here. I had to be off the streets tonight. I've been feeling full of a lot of anger and confusion, and that something is gonna come down, either to me or someone close to me. It's Friday night, so who knows what kind of hell I'd be getting into if I wasn't here. So I'm here to support my brothers, feed my soul, and focus my energy. I needed to be in my spirit and to be here tonight." His honesty touched us deeply. Several of the young men immediately acknowledged their respect for him and assured him that he was and would always be part of this circle.

David's sincerity created a miracle. Some of the guys who rarely spoke began to share. Because David disclosed a deep truth, they felt they could also confide their thoughts or feelings. There would be no judgments. Someone commented that he felt Antonio's spirit present. Possibly feeling the presence of spirit and carrying the fresh sorrow of Antonio's death, the group responded with a conversation about guns, why a few of them carried, and the craziness on the street. The heart words continued. I just listened.

A couple of the young men had been carrying guns since their early teens and were now acknowledging that it had to end because they were either going to be killed, or worse, they would kill someone else. Throughout the ceremony, the young men continued to acknowledge their respect for each other. They were proud that Rick was going to college, they were proud that Tomás was going into the navy, they were proud of how they had been there for each other. Later, as the fire burned low, we closed the circle with each person sharing their heart words with Tomás, a prayer, and then *abrazos* (hugs).

Most of the young men in the circle that evening found a place of deeper trust and respect among their peers where they could share their struggles, be heard, and have their honesty validated. As David was able to dissipate some of the anger consuming his heart, others were able to articulate difficult issues concerning their lives. One later expressed his belief that Antonio, the young man who had been murdered, was present in spirit, that he was able to observe the circle and draw gladness that his life was not lost in vain. He could smile because the circle had invited him to convey a message that had not been previously heard. A couple of the young men affirmed that their lives were too precious to continue carrying weapons and gave up their guns. All of the young men were so moved by this experience that they agreed to meet again for a council meeting, and the circle grew as other brothers and cousins were invited. And Tomás was able to leave for the navy feeling strong and powerful because he knew that his partners would continue caring about him.

Many years have passed since that circle, and I can clearly see the miracles that happened. Around the time of the ceremony, David had been struggling with guilt about being one of the few people in his group to survive the ghetto experience. Most of his childhood partners were living *"la vida loca"*—gang banging, selling drugs, and using drugs, and it was possible that he would have followed a similar path. Today, David and Rick are both highly recognized public school teachers. Both are working in the community in which they were raised, helping young people find a good path. When I asked David how he survived, he said, *"Familia, cultura,* our struggle, and *ceremonia* (the unity circle).[4] *Ceremonia* reminds me of my courage and power. It helps me focus my purpose and direction. There is lot of ugliness in the world, but *ceremonia* helps me realize that there is also beauty. This offers hope, which is absolutely essential to continue our progress."

When I asked a couple of the young men what miracles had happened for them that night, they told me:

- *I felt like I had a true family, brothers I could depend on and who could depend on me.*
- *I became more confident and secure because I knew I could say what I felt and the others would understand.*
- *I learned that ceremony can improve our communication by making us want to be more honest and positive.*
- *Images and feelings of the circle have stayed with me. There are times when I am down, but when I remember the circle and the burning sage, I know that I am not alone and that there is a lot of good in the world.*

This experience affected me as well. It helped me overcome my own prejudices about our youth on the street. It deepened my understanding that young people need opportunities to receive and show respect. Most of these young men were physically large and somewhat intimidating, rarely smiled, and at first glance might be judged as "gangster types." This experience reminded me that I shouldn't be quick to judge, that these young people were trying to survive in the best way they knew how.

My evening with them was a blessing and an honor. While the young men may not have been comfortable naming it as such, they exchanged and were touched by deep love. Everything about their lives on the street and among their peers required that they never show vulnerability or weakness. That night, they created the miracle of love, and demonstrated and strengthened their courage to be good men.

Besides the transformations that occurred for several of the young men that evening, the experience also contributed to them becoming a more connected *familia*. I am repeatedly inspired hearing about how they have maintained and expanded their circle into their own beloved community. They support each other. Now, some with children and others not, they assist each other in being conscious teachers and role models for the kids, to foster their self-confidence and teach values about family and community. They are not always perfect, but they often do remind each other about being their best, and I have seen them support each other in various activist and community projects.

Unity circles offer men a place where trust and respect can grow.

Because of the miracles that can come from bringing people together for meaningful sharing, we need more people to initiate unity or sharing circles among families and friends. Initially many have thoughts like, "I can't do it, I'm not that spiritual, I could never speak to a group." If these have been your considerations, I ask that you discard them as old insecurities limiting your power. Trust that if you feel even the least desire or calling to do this work, you can do it, and many people will reflect their love and support back to you for having the courage to step forward.

The Men's Council: Time to Feed the Soul

While experiences like unity circles and other meaningful family gatherings can inspire insights and even commitments to change, most of us need something more regular to support our ability to be the change we desire. We need regular conversations or meetings to support us with the ongoing learning and affirmation necessary to continue living the path of transformation. Here the council, the tradition of ongoing meetings for mutual sharing and support, is a tremendous resource. While the council story presented below involves men meeting in a manner that draws from our indigenous tradition, councils can be organized by and for men, women, and youth of all cultures or interests.

I recently retrieved a message from my answering machine from Ignacio, a young single father: "Just calling to say, I won the custody case for my children. Everyone said I'm doing a great job with the kids. My thanks to you and the men's council. You have all sustained me these past two years. I couldn't have done it without everyone's counsel and support." Ignacio's gratitude echoed the words of many others who have participated in our Oakland Men's Council over the past twenty years.

During the late 1970s, I collaborated with folks from a number of related community networks to organize councils to aid us in supporting each other in living the values of love and community action. The councils were composed of people committed to sharing dialogue and support while using tools from our "indigenous council tradition." For a number of years, I cofacilitated several councils that brought together family, friends, and colleagues to assist each other to live and work in a *porvida* way to foster love and transformation in all our actions. At one point, Ron Chavez, a *compadre* dedicated to community building, confided that he—and he believed, other men—needed a men's council to support our growth as *hombres de corazón* (men guided by the heart). We collaborated in organizing a men's retreat in January 1987 that resulted in a men's council that has been meeting on the first Friday of the month ever since.

Our initial retreat involved more than twenty mostly Latino men who were dedicated to community service. As we continued meeting, thirteen of those men became regular participants, coming together to discern what it means to be "men guided by the heart" while exploring the issues that restrained our transformative potential. Our group was kept semiclosed to strengthen the trust required for deep spiritual exploration and personal growth. For many of us who carried major leadership responsibilities in the community, this circle became a safe haven for sharing vulnerabilities, and learning from each other wisdom for being good fathers, sons, and community leaders. Repeatedly, members expressed that they were there "to drink from the well," to feed their soul, and to share their experience with others who might benefit.

As original members left, friends and others desiring to share support were invited to join the council. After eleven years, it became apparent that many others could also benefit from the medicine of dialogue and the spirit of community we shared within the council. Consequently, we decided to become a more open council and extended an invitation to a number of young men whom we viewed as future leaders.

Now, after twenty years, the Oakland Men's Council has evolved to be a truly multigenerational group, mostly Latinos, yet also multicultural.[5] One of our charter documents well reflects the group's purpose: "We believe that healthy individuals are needed to create healthy families and a healthy world. We come together to create sacred space to nurture our spirit and support each other's growth. We join together as men with the purpose to evolve our humanness, our spirituality, and our ability to be 'healer/warriors' in the world."

Two years ago, Ignacio was invited to one of our council sessions. During the introductory sharing round in which everyone offers a brief version of "what is going great or what is challenging in your life," Ignacio shared his confusion. He felt he was on the verge of a separation from his wife and wanted to move forward in a responsible way for his young children (ages two and four years). His wife had been supportive of him during his university studies and he was attempting to do the same for her. However, during her studies she moved away, leaving him to assume primary parenting responsibilities. He expressed the conflict he felt almost every evening holding his children as they cried, wanting to know when mommy was coming home. Ignacio's struggle involved not wanting to say anything negative about mommy, but also feeling his own pain and frustration. Feeling his anguish, members of the council extended support and friendship, and assured him that whenever he attended council, he would have time to voice his feelings and discuss his difficulties. If desired, we would offer our reflections, validations, and prayers.

Despite complexities that continued to surface within Ignacio's family, there were also times to rejoice over victories Ignacio was experiencing as a committed father. One time he took his children to a march for immigrant rights, and his son asked why everyone was walking together. Ignacio responded, "We want all people to live a better life." Later his son expressed pride to his dad that they were continuing to march for justice like César Chávez had done years before. Over time, Ignacio continued to share difficult challenges and invite counsel from the other men, just as many of us had been doing for each other, teaching all of us how to be more loving fathers, uncles, and sons.

Councils can be facilitated in many forms, and there are no strict requirements, provided the essential goal to support each other's growth is honored. The Oakland Men's Council uses the following format. We gather once a month at a set time, and commence with a traditional honoring of the four directions done with burning sage and sharing prayers. The session then begins with each member offering brief words about their life realities. This initial *conocimiento* typically surfaces potential themes or questions for the evening. These may include matters raised during the prior gathering or new issues, and vary from how to be supportive of rebellious children to how to be an agent of change within one's extended family or workplace. At times personal issues that need to be heard and supported become our first concern. The themes for the evening are selected by the group, and the designated facilitator serves to maintain the focus. Over the years, these dialogues have resulted in many miracles as members discharge the stresses of their lives, gain insights on dealing with family and work matters, revive their commitment to community activism, or experience the healing of receiving or extending prayers. More about the principles used to guide our meetings is elaborated in "Constants for Our Gatherings," presented below.

The foremost perspective shared by the group is that the selfishness, materialism, and exploitation prevalent in our society must be transformed. The council is our means to encourage love and move this transformation, beginning with ourselves and our family and friends. We are inspired by the courage demonstrated by each other and the knowledge that there are many other councils similar to ours occurring around the country that also support growth, empowerment, and dedicated action to better our world.[6]

MEN'S COUNCIL:

CONSTANTS FOR OUR GATHERINGS

We meet in the tradition of Chicano men's councils, which welcome all men committed to personal development, social justice, respect for our earth, and peace in our world. Our meetings are guided by the following principles.[7]

1. **Honor the council as sacred time and place.**
   - Come with the intention of honoring each other and the Creator by listening attentively and sharing our truths.
2. **Create a collective center.**
   - Form the circle and an altar to focus the group energy.
3. **Open with gratitude and invitation.**
   - Begin with sage burning, and prayers to the Creator and your ancestors. These prayers include words of gratitude, recognition and invitation, and requests for support and guidance.
4. **Nurture our relationship as community.**
   - Provide for *conocimiento* to reaffirm trust and bring all voices to the circle.
   - Continue the relationships of mutual support outside the circle.
5. **Share our experience to feel, heal, and learn.**
   - Listen with and speak from the heart; speak with respect and love.
   - Communicate your experience to reclaim your ability to feel, and to permit the members to learn from each other.

6. **Support and share leadership.**
   - All share the responsibility to encourage the participation of all members and to support the designated leader's facilitation.
7. **End with gratitude.**
   - End councils with words of gratitude to the Creator and to each other.

PRAXIS

1. Are there friends whom you would like to recognize as family? What benefits could you see in formally recognizing your bond as uncle, aunt, nephew, niece, or cousin? What type of ceremony, small or large, can you envision that would honor and support your wish to create family in this way?

2. What benefits might you see for yourself, and for others, in having available a support group such as the men's council? Could you envision initiating such a council? What would be your purpose? How could you initiate its organization?

3. Create an opportunity to share one of these stories with a group of family or friends, and then have a conversation. Ask them for their insights and feelings, and how you might apply these tools within your circles or networks. The group's ideas will be many, so prioritize a few and support each other in their implementation.

13

EXPANDING FAMILY ACTION INTO COMMUNITY ACTION

● ●

By applying the *Familia* Approach, we can all increase our ability to create positive influence in the world. We can facilitate experiences that foster joy and love within our families, while nurturing values that make us more caring people ready to serve our communities. We can create beloved and empowered community with family and friends who support each other as we pursue the evolution of our culture and the betterment of society. We can do all this when we have a clear vision, and believe in ourselves and our strategy.

Earlier, I described how multiple actions are often necessary to achieve our desired outcomes. Our vision of a better society actually involves a constellation of desired outcomes that begins with more empowered and caring individuals and families, who in turn can influence positive change among their communities and beyond. The effort we invest in our family networks is but one of the influences required to actualize this larger vision, which ultimately must involve hundreds of thousands of families participating in community service and action. Yet it is essential that we fully recognize that what we do in our family networks can lead to other activist actions, and this is even more possible when we have in mind what those other actions look like.

This chapter provides examples of how dedicated family activism applied among our friends or work groups can make real the vision we have for our society. I say "dedicated" family activism because the changes we desire often require years of effort. In each example, the positive influences of becoming and acting as an empowered and beloved community grew over several years. In one case a group of families influenced the youth, schools, and greater community of their city, and in another a group of people became like an activist family and are advancing the transformation of a museum that is influencing the culture of an entire region. Both of these stories are followed by a list of various practices and actions that illustrate how we can direct our numerous daily actions toward a clear purpose with powerful cumulative effects.

There are a couple more stories intended to convey other possibilities and lessons. While it often takes years for family or community groups to create the impacts we desire, the time we spend working together can be a piece of heaven on Earth—developing relationships of trust and respect while enjoying each other's companionship and children. In turn, the familiarity and trust we develop sometimes enable us to seize opportunities to make meaningful contributions to change. Because of the years that one of my family networks spent in being *familia*, it took us only weeks to assist in convening a local peace initiative. Similarly, because of years that another group of friends spent being family with each other, they were able to initiate in a few months a project that registered more than 20,000 new women voters for the 2004 election.

Transforming an Institution by Becoming More *Familia*

Family activists can draw on the values of family to assist organizations to more powerfully serve the community and facilitate positive change. The Days of the Dead tradition celebrated by the Latino community during the end of October and the beginning of November has its origins in Mexico, and has been evolved by Mexican-Americans as a time to honor deceased loved ones with family and community altars and celebrations. Given my professional experience supporting people who have lost loved ones, and the death of my younger brother, Jack, to AIDS, I grew to appreciate the power of this tradition for helping families heal the loss of loved ones.[1] Its healing character prompted me to pursue evolving this tradition to encourage people to live more committed to being their best. This

Maya sharing about her grandfather at a family Days of the Dead celebration.

vision came to mind when I learned how the people of South Africa, who were only allowed to meet in public to bury their dead, used their memorial services to inspire the community action necessary to end apartheid.

I saw that we needed to inform and demonstrate to our greater Latino community the power and potential of the Days of the Dead tradition, and that we needed an organization to assist us. After considering various possibilities, several friends and I decided to pursue making the Oakland Museum of California our partner, as the museum was just then reaching out to the Latino community. Soon, along with other interested Latinos, we began building the Latino Advisory Committee, whose mission was to help the museum become more responsive to the needs and vision of the local community. After some time, an informal opportunity arose for several of us to create for the public a unity circle to celebrate the Days of the Dead. Museum staff and other participants were so deeply touched by the feelings of spirit and community kindled by this event that they enthusiastically embraced the vision of developing a program to share this tradition with the community on an ongoing basis. Over just a couple of years, we developed an annual exhibit and community celebration program that now touches many thousands of people.

Every year, hundreds of volunteers and staff become like family to advance an understanding and practice of the Days of the Dead as a form of healing, spiritual growth, family nurturance, inspiration, and community building. More than 17,000 people from all cultures, mostly young people, come to the exhibits, workshops, and the community celebration each year. There they learn ways to appreciate different cultural traditions and to honor their deceased loved ones. Of these visitors, nearly 4,000 participate in the annual community celebration, which includes a special unity circle to honor loved ones by remembering their gifts and committing to live their positive values. Many people bring family and friends to experience the inspirational quality of this celebration.[2]

The unique approach we have developed at the Oakland Museum builds on old and new traditions to advance the Days of the Dead as a force for community building, cultural evolution, and transformation. By using the tools of family activism from the onset of our work, we developed within the Latino Advisory Committee, the Days of the Dead Committee, and museum staff a culture of active *conocimiento*, mutual appreciation, empowerment, and community building.[3] By utilizing vision, facilitation, unity circles, and ceremony, the groups continue to demonstrate the power of beloved community by supporting each other as family as we work to advance greater community well-being.

One of the projects inspired by the Days of the Dead program was the "100 Families of Oakland" program, which involves Oakland families creating art to better know themselves and their communities. A powerful altar installation at the 2003 Days of the Dead exhibit that focused on the 114 homicides in Oakland the year before inspired a philanthropist to initiate this program. Families from four of the communities most affected by these tragedies were invited to participate in creating art together, with the goal of strengthening their family and neighborhood and reducing violence. The museum exhibit that resulted from this effort, "100 Families of Oakland: Art and Social Change," has now inspired a number of other cities to initiate similar programs.[4]

Drawing learning and inspiration from our Days of the Dead experience, key museum staff sought to take that same spirit of *familia*, multicultural respect, and innovation to the larger museum organization. In 2002, I was invited by the associate director to work with the curatorial staff and then the management team to do team building and plan for innovation. In essence, we applied the principles of family activism to foster a spirit of vision and community within the entire institution. Since then, all these influences have worked together to inspire further transformation of the museum and many other projects committed to supporting community well-being and multicultural respect.

 FAMILY ACTIVIST

PRACTICES

The following are examples of key family activist practices that I and others employed while supporting the Latino Advisory Committee. Which ones can you see yourself utilizing?

- We initiated a meeting tradition of doing *conocimiento*. We began every meeting by sharing what was going on in our lives, thus developing relationships among members and staff that inspired everyone to contribute more to ensuring the success of our projects.
- We developed as a committee norm a commitment to support the leadership development of other committee members and staff. The result was that we became highly successful in maintaining a focus on vision, facilitating effective meetings, being innovative, and building community.

- We incorporated into our committee work times for ceremony and unity circles to maintain a consciousness of spirit and our commitment to advance positive change for our communities, today and for "seven generations."

- We organized and encouraged committee members and supporters to participate in informal gatherings, such as holiday dinners, to nurture connection among ourselves and our families.

- We collaborated with other museum cultural communities to continually foster an inclusive sense of multicultural community and a joint commitment to create a better world.

- We sought to practice and model the values we desire to see in our society. This involved treating each other with respect, validating each other's efforts, and sometimes providing each other constructive feedback.

From Friends to an Activist Family

Beloved community consists of people who support each other as friends and in their actions to create positive change. When you are living as beloved community, you are giving attention to each other's children, learning from each other, and applying time to make community life better for your family and others. The following is about our experience of living as beloved community with other families during the time we lived in Castro Valley, yet the story begins in our new home in Ventura, California.

Young Carlos, the son of family friends, arrived at our new home at a perfect time. It was my wife's birthday, and the entire city of Ventura was celebrating their fall arts festival and Days of the Dead. Carlos joined our group of family and friends in touring the street fair and then in sharing dinner. By the end of the evening, several adults expressed how they were inspired by this young man, an environmental biologist and aspiring yoga teacher who radiated love, respect, and maturity. I smiled, recalling a number of incidents that led up to this moment beginning with the efforts of a group of parents in Castro Valley to build an organization to advance multicultural respect and the success of our children. It was this organization which had awarded Carlos the scholarship that had affirmed his goal to become an environmental activist. The network of relationships and the cycle of positive influence had all started with a phone call.

In 1995, Elsa, a concerned mother, called me, outraged at the school administration and the local sheriff's department. She informed me that a sheriff's officer had recently delivered a presentation on gang violence at the middle school parents meeting that appalled her as it unjustly characterized many Latinos as gang suspects. Concerned about the negative impact of such images, Elsa wanted to organize a meeting of parents to address the officer's racist portrayal of Latinos and to possibly recommend that the officer be reprimanded. Affirming her concern, while questioning her desired outcome, I told her that I would attend if she secured the commitment of a group of parents.

Elsa gathered nearly twenty parents, most of whom did not know each other. During introductions, Elsa shared her view that we organize to meet with the sheriff's department regarding our concerns. But before we pursued this line of action, I asked the group if we could first talk about what we ideally wanted for our children. My consideration was the organizing principle that one should clarify vision and purpose before developing strategies. Having already hung easel paper on the wall, I prompted the group to brainstorm a vision for our children's education. Parents expressed several desires they held, including high school graduation, preparation for college, an experience of respect, learning about their culture, leadership development, and giving back to their community. Then I asked the parents where they preferred to focus our time, on exploring how to advance our vision or on communicating with the sheriff's department. By the conclusion of our meeting, the group of parents decided to be proactive and become the Castro Valley Latino Education Association and build an organization to support the success of our children.[5] A committee was also formed to communicate our concern to increase multicultural respect from the school district and the sheriff's department.

Over the next ten years, we became a family of friends, getting to know each other's children, along with their friends and teachers, as we initiated a number of school activities and programs that had a profound influence on hundreds, if not thousands, of students and parents. While we periodically went to the school administration with our concerns, we typically set forth our goals and made them happen through our collective volunteerism. We sponsored annual cultural events surrounding the Days of the Dead, Christmas, and *Cinco de Mayo*. These events familiarized our children with their culture and engaged others in multicultural experiences that expanded their awareness and respect. We became the support group for the high school Latino student association and initiated a leadership development program for students at the high school.

Two particular activities sponsored by our group had tremendous impact upon students and the school community. The first was an annual Days of the Dead dinner celebration. As explained earlier, the Days of the Dead are a time when Mexican-Americans honor ancestors and loved ones who have died. We developed a fundraising celebration centered around a unity circle ceremony that brought many of our city's activists and education leaders together to honor deceased loved ones by recommitting to better our community and our world in their remembrance. The outcome was deep community building, as activist parents, teachers, and principals of all cultures became more connected. Invariably, the conversations that followed our ceremony set in motion partnerships and initiatives to make our schools better for our students.

The other event that had a significant community impact was our *Cinco de Mayo* (Fifth of May) essay-writing contest. We universalized the celebration of *Cinco de Mayo* to invite all high school students to write essays about "victories despite opposition," which reflects the underlying theme of this Mexican-American celebration. Students were invited to write about a personal or family experience of achieving goals despite tremendous struggle. The response was always amazing, as we would receive dozens of powerful essays from the school's multicultural student body. Their writings included stories of personal triumph, the achievements of parents and ancestors who struggled to create a better life for their children, and of intimate family experiences, such as an uncle inspiring those around him while living his final months with AIDS.

Every year scholarships were awarded to the contest winners at a special evening program where these students read their essays. One year, among the winners was a young person who surprised many peers and parents, given his reputation as a member of an irresponsible party crowd. Yet his essay about his family's tradition of community responsibility and his vision of making a difference as an environmental scientist inspired many of us. Now, six years later, living 350 miles way from the city where we met, Carlos has repeatedly found time to visit us. He visits because we have become family, through the relationship his father and I developed as fellow activist members of the parent association, and also because I have been available to listen to him at critical times when he was struggling with college life.

Carlos's visits remind me of the family network we developed as members of the Castro Valley Latino Education Association. For more than ten years we were part of a community of a dozen families encouraging leadership development among our youth and multicultural respect within our greater community. We were there for each other during fun and challenging times, often acting as caring friends and family. Many of our group's children came to view each other's parents, including Rebeca and me, as aunts or uncles. We were an organization of parents advocating and organizing to ensure a quality educational experience for our children, and together we had also become the village that cared for our children.

The birth and success of our parents association was a product of family activism. Elsa initiated the organization because of her concern regarding how Latinos were being portrayed within the schools. Then, from the beginning, I applied the tools of the *Familia* Approach to foster relationships of deep connection. Quickly, the group integrated the practice of doing *conocimiento* in virtually all of our activities, and we developed a reputation for having an inviting and mutually supportive culture. People participated in our activities because the group felt like family and community. We also learned to use vision to focus and optimize our energy, practiced facilitation skills to guide successful meetings, employed co-powering techniques to support and empower each other, and shared numerous unity circles to reinspire our commitment to our family and community. We became a beloved community that made being a force for love and positive change enjoyable for ourselves and our families.

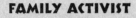 **FAMILY ACTIVIST**

PRACTICES

The following are examples of some key family activist practices I and others employed while supporting the network of Castro Valley parents. Which ones have you employed in your family and community?

- We provided parents at the initial meeting an opportunity to reframe their concerns and consider their greater vision: success for their students.
- We committed to doing *conocimiento* at all our meetings to get to know each other and nurture our relationship as community. We encouraged parents to engage in one-to-one *conocimiento* sessions outside our meetings to better know and support each other.
- We offered support and challenged each other to contribute our best and focus our efforts.
- We reached out to develop supportive relationships with young people.
- We encouraged each other to explore the use of our cultural traditions to organize community, raise self-esteem, and encourage multicultural understanding.
- We collaborated with other parents to sponsor formal and informal events to foster community building among children, youth, parents, and families.

- We drew on such traditions as the unity circle to inspire ourselves and others to embrace our higher purpose and goals—to advance love, multicultural respect, success for all students, and more.

Mobilizing for Peace

I still hear from some activists, "What relevance do family gatherings have with the actions required to stop global warming or the war in Iraq?" It's true that in and of themselves enjoyable family gatherings may contribute little to improving our society directly. Yet each gathering can serve to build relationships, inspire, and inform others so that at the right time they can be mobilized to engage in significant acts of community service or protest. One example is the peace demonstrations that occurred in Oakland, California, during March 2006.

Hundreds of Oakland elementary and high school students will long remember the actions they took for peace on March 27, 2006. It was the first time students of several schools ever participated in a peace rally. And for at least forty high school students, it was the day they made the courageous decision to leave campus and join a major peace march demonstrating through their city.

A number of events led up to this day when students from five Oakland schools participated in learning about and standing for peace. Two of the main influences were Latinos for Peace, an organization formed by families of the greater Oakland area, and the 241 Miles March for Peace initiative started by Fernando Suárez del Sol and family, whose son was killed at age twenty in the first week of the war in Iraq.

For more than thirty years Eduardo García had been a member of the dozen and a half families informally called *Nueva Familia* (New Family). The network began during the early 1970s when a number of college students moved into the area and connected with local activists involved in community service. Together we formed a beloved community of people committed to supporting each other and making Oakland a better place for all people. Over the years, as we married and became godparents or informal aunts and uncles to each other's children, we made our gatherings opportunities for joyful connection. We also frequently collaborated with each other on projects to ensure quality education for our children.

It was in the kitchen at one of these family celebrations that Eduardo declared to a few of us that the war in Iraq was outrageously wrong and it was our responsibility to raise a voice for peace. Drawing mostly on our family network, the first meeting of Latinos for Peace was held a few weeks later. We began by identifying current antiwar and peace activities to determine how to best make our contribution. As other organizations were already involved in various community education peace activities, we decided to give our energy to supporting others.

When an appeal came to support Fernando Suárez del Sol and his peace march from Tijuana to San Francisco, our group mobilized. Ever since his son had been killed in Iraq, Fernando had been urging communities throughout the country to recognize how the military establishment uses young people and undocumented immigrants to fight and die in a war that must be ended. Members of Latinos for Peace took significant responsibility for the Oakland portion of the march, which included holding mini–peace rallies at several schools, followed by another at a local community college.

The peace rallies at each school were uniquely different and inspiring. At the first school the marchers were blessed by nuns and more than eighty students standing on the front steps of the school, each holding one hand over his or her heart and the other hand stretched out to extend prayers to the marchers. Arriving at the next school, we were welcomed by a crowd of hundreds of elementary school students waving placards for peace. At this rally, we coached the youngsters on how to raise the issue of peace in their homes with their parents and families. A similar experience occurred at the next elementary school.

Our big surprise occurred at the high school rally. Here, people like Camilo Mejía, the first Iraq war veteran to file for a discharge from the army as a conscientious objector, spoke. Given what he had seen after six months of combat, he had concluded that he could not continue to support an illegal and immoral war and decided not to

It is our responsibility to raise a voice for peace.

return, a decision that resulted in a year in the stockade. His courageous story inspired several students to take the microphone. Student speakers connected the issue of the war to the oppressive treatment of Latinos, who are urged to fight for this nation while being treated as criminals for working without documents. They also questioned the relevancy of remaining in school on this day when they could partake in creating history. By the time we left the school more than forty students departed with us.

Many of the high school students who joined the march expressed fear regarding the repercussions of leaving campus, yet they had a sense of profound correctness in taking a stand to make a difference. As we conversed about the meaning of their action, it was clear that for many this day was a defining moment in their lives when they chose a higher commitment—to take action to advance justice for all.

No one can gauge the various outcomes that will occur because of the peace march and rallies that day, but I do know that years of community connection and orientation to social justice that we had nurtured within our *familia* events had led to Latinos for Peace and the peace rally. In part, this day had occurred because several of us had applied our activism over the years to make our family network a beloved community capable of community action.

There are activists who focus on getting people out for major community-building events and protest activities. Their work is absolutely necessary and must be supported. Similarly, we must validate the activism that occurs when others, often women, do the inviting, food preparation, and facilitating to bring family and friends together to become closer community. These seemingly modest efforts can over time foster the strength and resilience that enable family and friends to step up when called upon to participate in community service or protest actions.

A Retreat Center for Activists and 20,000 New Voters

Many of us are part of family and friend networks that seem to have happened spontaneously. Certain people sought to be among other good people and they became community. How much more powerful could these networks become if more members nurtured them as communities capable of greater collaborative action? Some of the accomplishments of the North Brier Family Network cited below may help provide an answer. Here, an informal community of families has achieved tremendous accomplishments without any explicit consciousness of family activism, yet in many ways they are modeling the best of the family activist tradition.

At a family retreat center in the hills above the Russian River in northern California, twelve staff of the Rockwood Leadership Program met to refine their strategy to provide the best training possible to leaders of nonprofit organizations throughout the country.[6] During the weeks that followed, similar organizations, such as Ruckus and Rainforest Action Network, also held staff retreats there to plan strategies to advance their goals for community betterment and environmental protection. This special retreat center sprung out of the living room dialogues of a group of friends we are going to call the North Brier Family Network, as, given their informality up to this time, they didn't have a name.

While working at Greenpeace, André Carothers identified his desire to combine his passion for environmental protection with the joy of working with great people, so he recruited onto the team his close companions from high school. The friendships continued deepening, and when one friend left for California, the others followed with the common vision of buying houses next to each other to maintain their connection. This group of friends attracted other progressive people, until they became over a half dozen families linked by common backyards and the joy of supporting each other and helping care for their children.

They did not consciously apply the approach of family activism, yet the commitment and practice of mutual support and community service was always present. Friends were supporting each other, talking politics and vision, and collaborating on projects of common interest.

As the friends had children, the idea repeatedly surfaced of owning a place together that could serve as a retreat getaway for their families and friends. Finally someone said, let's do it, and contacted an agent who located a ranch for sale named Black Mountain. The close relationship that existed among a number of the families enabled them to generate an agreement regarding the purchase, and later to develop a plan to build a space for group meetings with adjoining sleeping units. For the last several years, Black Mountain Ranch has served both these families and the progressive organizations they desire to support.

This same group of friends often shared strategies for making our nation more responsible. Several of these conversations about the need for a new president led to a living room meeting of a handful of friends that in time grew to meetings of more than twenty people. This larger group began to consider how to generate the greatest impact on the upcoming election with the least investment of time. The group learned that 22 million single women did not vote in the 2000 election, and that 16 million of those women didn't even register to vote. The group determined that if these women registered and voted in 2004, they could determine the next president. Given this insight, the group developed a Web-based organization to strategically reach out to hair, nail, and beauty salons across the nation to make them venues for activating single women to register and vote.

Their campaign, called "1000 Flowers," built a network of volunteers, salons, and businesses interested in empowering women voters and registered an estimated 20,000 new voters. Because of their efforts and those of many other organizations with a similar mission, more than 7 million more single women voters turned out to vote than in the 2000 election.[7]

The potential for future collaborations is unlimited, yet even more encouraging is the manner in which the family network members support each other's success. Each of the nearly twenty members of the North Brier Family Network brings to the group their own experience, talents, and network connections, which include staff or board member relationships with more than two dozen nonprofit organizations. This makes the group an invaluable resource for supporting each other and creating opportunities for collaboration. André explains, "Within our network, emerging opportunities, management challenges, technical issues, campaign turning points, and personal issues are always surfacing. It's fantastic that we are repeatedly able to assist each other to achieve significant personal and organizational successes. We do it by drawing upon each other. The work becomes more satisfying, and easier, when you know where to turn when issues come up. Whether it's for information, expertise, or counsel, we turn to each other because the confidentiality, familiarity, confidence, and expertise are established."[8]

While acknowledging the significance of the activist and professional resources provided by his familial network, what appears to enthuse André most are the relationships the families share. His children and the children of his friends see each other as family and regard the adults as uncles and aunts. To André, all the facilitation he has done among the families has never felt deliberate, but instinctive: "I never really thought about it, I just did my part and we did the rest."

The accomplishments of the North Brier Family Network provide an important lesson to many of us already engaged in family activism. Maybe, given our caring commitment, we just call it being good friends, neighbors, or community. Maybe we don't even call it anything because it is simply how we choose to live—to be family with each other. We support all those around us to be and contribute their best because that is what family, and family activism, is all about.

PRAXIS

1. All the illustrations involved being beloved community, family, and friends committed to supporting each other and creating change. If you are part of such a community or potential community, how can you help strengthen its abilities? If you are not part of such a network, where or how can you begin developing key relationships of mutual support that can grow your community?

2. The Oakland Museum committee and the Castro Valley parent group drew on cultural traditions to support their organizing activities. In each case, special cultural occasions were expanded to make them more inclusive and inspiring for all people. How might we apply this approach with Earth Day, Martin Luther King Jr. Day, Valentine's Day, Independence Day, Mother's Day, or other holidays? Consider one of these occasions and outline in several bullet points how one might make it an opportunity to build community or to inspire community service or action. If the idea you developed interests you, whom could you bring together to evolve the possibilities and to possibly follow through with action?

CONCLUSION:
PRAXIS AND BLESSINGS

The nature of praxis is that we do our best to contribute to growth and change, and then afterward, at least for a few moments, we savor and reflect on our experience for the inspiration and learning it can provide us. I wish to share a few such moments with you now.

My praxis for the activism involved in completing this book begins with extending my profound appreciation to you for investing the time to learn tools that can make you a more empowering resource for your family and our communities. Even in the process of learning, you are contributing energy to the Great Turning. I would be glad to hear of your achievements and learnings regarding family activism, via robertovargas.com.

This writing experience has aided me in clarifying the tools involved in family activism, the importance of this activism, and the need for you and me to take these tools to the next level. For more than twenty-five years, I have sought to develop my networks of family and friends, mostly to create for us a community that supports our collective happiness, success, and activism, and to learn more about family activism. Much of what I learned I either applied in my consultation or organizing work or sought to teach by modeling. Not until the preparation of this book was I forced to explain principles and practices that were still rather intuitive. I was like a self-taught cook who, after many years of preparing complex meals, now sought to spell out the recipes and directions in writing. Responding to this challenge has taught me more about what I know—and what I wish to learn.

The co-powering message is reflected in Andrea's art. This watercolor painting titled ¡Si, Se Puede! captures Oakland youth chanting that "Yes, we can make positive change."

I want to learn more about co-powering communications. I want to identify *conocimiento* questions that can be used to help family and friends more strongly connect with their power to support family and engage in the activism of change. I want to learn more about using our family conversations to develop a mature understanding of our social reality and transformation, and other ways to foster social consciousness. I want to learn more about how to move families from sharing love and inspiration with each other to engaging in more strategic community action directed to changing institutions, advocacy efforts, community self-help, political campaigns, and other initiatives for change. And I want to learn more about how to activate people, and how to encourage people to live up to their own community service goals.

While working on the book, I have spoken with many new acquaintances about family activism. The discussions have been affirming and inspiring. Repeatedly, people have voiced their excitement about the idea of family activism because it inspires hope and affirms their commitments. A father who is actively involved in supporting political campaigns said he needed to hear validation for spending more time with his children because he was feeling guilty about doing less of the "more important political work." Similarly, a physician whose life is overly full serving people with AIDS and caring for her two young children expressed how wonderful it felt to recognize that dedicating time to her children is also being socially responsible. These and other conversations pointed to the importance of balance, cultivating healthy families, and developing our children to become confident, caring, and activist people.

People remarked that we could become a powerful social change movement if we incorporated the principles of family activism within our community service and political action organizations. We need to develop more family and community values within our service organizations to attract others, to sustain those who are involved, and to actually be the change we desire in the world.

These conversations were uplifting and, sometimes, frustrating. Uplifting because they reaffirmed the importance of family activism to sustain our commitment and create our desired cultural transformation. Frustrating because they made apparent the enormous need for additional organizations and tools to sustain those already involved in family activism, and those who need to learn these skills to support their family and communities.

Family activism is an art form still in its early stages. While we can apply the methods of family activism, we need to further evolve these tools and strategies for social-action–oriented community building, organizing, and advocacy. I believe that as we mature as activists, we will develop new and powerful ways to support each other in building a society that works for all. If so, the emerging movement for living *porvida* love will blossom.

I again extend my prayers and blessings to you for your commitment and service.

- May you and yours be blessed with much health and wisdom.
- May we create for ourselves and our families great lives of happiness and service.

- May we find the ways to transform the selfishness, fear, and irresponsible institutions that limit our individual and social potential.
- May we do our part to restore and advance the well-being of Mother Earth and our human family.

ACKNOWLEDGMENTS

● ●

This book is a product of the loving relationships shared by many people. This web of family and community connection began with my grandmother, Mama Cuca, who taught me about family, joy, and power. My mother followed by modeling her practice of community service. My gratitude is then extended to everyone whom I have experienced as family for the inspiration, challenges, and support they have brought me.

I am also grateful to the many friends and colleagues who collaborated with me over the years to create institutions, organizations, and networks committed to advocacy and community service. Heartfelt thanks to the many family and friends who similarly collaborated to create councils for learning, teaching, and modeling the practice of *porvida* leadership and family activism. Together, we inspired and clarified much of the wisdom foundational to family activism.

For the development and production of this book itself, I feel a deep sense of gratitude:

To Rebeca, my wife, for being an active partner in living the principles of love and service within our multiple family circles.

To my entire family, particularly my mother, Tita, daughters Andrea and Ixchel, brothers Art and Marcos, their wives and children, and our godchildren for willingly allowing me to share our family experiences to provide illustrations that could benefit others.

To many of my extended family for also permitting me to draw from our experience to share illustrations that teach the power of

Roberto visiting with Mama Cuca and nephew in Torreon, Mexico, 1974.

family councils and unity circles, particularly the Soto family and the García families.

To friends and colleagues who over the years have encouraged me to assume this writing task, particularly Eduardo Salaz, John and Judith Ratcliff, Ron Chavez, Puanani Burgess, Binnie Kristal Anderson, David C. Korten, Grace Lee Boggs, Sylvia Castillo, Christina Gonzalez, and Penelope Hughes.

To friends who gave of their time to read and comment on the evolving work, particularly Sergio García, Barbara Marquez, Canek Peña-Vargas, and Liz Miramontes.

To friends who were the early collaborators in developing the ideas foundational to family activism, including Francisco M. Hernandez, Yolanda Ronquillo, Samuel Martinez, and Vercila Chacon; and to the staff of *Casa del Sol* (*La Clinica de la Raza* Mental Health Department, Oakland, California) and *La Familia* Counseling Services (Hayward, California) who continue the practice of counseling with attentionn to family and community empowerment.

To the many people and organizations with whom I have shared a commitment to develop empowered and proactive communities. Our reciprocal support enabled our development of organizational cultures directed to positive change. In particular, I extend gratitude to Building Opportunities for Self-Sufficiency (boona cheema), Cabrillo Economic Development Corporation (Kathryn Benner, Priscila Cisneros, and Silvia Rodriguez), California Association for Bilingual Education (María Quezada), California State University at Long Beach (David Ramirez, Kim-Oanh Nguyen-Lam, and Cheryl Eames), Center for Excellence in Native Hawaiian Law (Susan Serrano and Eric Yamamoto), Equal Justice Society (Eva Paterson), Catholic Charities of the East Bay (Barbara Terrazas), Housing Authority of the City of Alameda (Mike Pucci), Hualapi Indian Reservation (Sandra Yellowhawk), Independent Media Institute (Don Hazen), Kaiser Permanente Latino Association (Edgar Quiroz), LatinosConnect@Intuit (María Arellano and Eduardo Salaz), Lawyers Committee for Civil Rights, Mills College (Romeo García), National Hispanic Employee Association (Frank Alvarez), Oakland Museum of California (Mark Medeiros and Barbara Henry), Rio Hondo College (Martha Carreon), Rockwood Leadership Program (Andre Carothers), Santa Clara County Supervisor Blanca Alvarado, Silicon Graphics (Deb Dagit), Somos Mayfair (Jaime Alvarado), Teatro Visión (Raul Lozano and Elisa Marina Alvarado), Tiburcio Vasquez Health Center (José Joél García), Yes! A Journal of Positive Futures (Fran Korten), and School of Social Welfare, University of California at Berkeley (Joseph Solis).

To Shams Kairys for his dedicated editing and moral support. Writing this book became incredibly more doable knowing his commitment and amazing talent were ever present to ensure that the message would communicate and our project would be completed.

To the entire team at Berrett-Koehler Publishers for their enthusiasm and support to make fhis book possible, particularly Johanna Vonderling, my senior editor, for our regular conference calls and her inspiring positivism; Jeevan Sivasubramaniam, my managing editor, for his dedicated commitment to the success of this project from the first hour we met; Dianne Platner and her design team for their persistence in finding a cover that worked; and Steve Piersanti, founder and publisher, for bringing together such a fine and dedicated team.

To the network of reviewers organized by Berrett-Koehler to provide feedback to help strengthen this work, including Gary M. Nelson, Onnesha Roychaoudhuri, Jeevan Sivasubramaniam, and Gabriela Melano. My deepest gratitude to Gabriela for her rigorous and loving treatment of my manuscript that made my rewriting a tremendous learning experience about the tools of family activism and myself.

Finally, to Linda Jupiter and her team for their creativity in ensuring the excellent internal look of the book and in preparing the book for printing, including Gopa Campbell, text designer; Henrietta Bensussen, proofreader; Medea Minnich, indexer; and especially, Lunaea Weatherstone for her attentive and careful copyediting.

NOTES

● ●

Preface

1. The inner symbol, popular within the ancient Aztec and Mayan cultures, is the ollin, which means "movement," and here is surrounded by flower petals. The images have been brought together by Chicano healers to underscore the type of leadership required today—people drawing the best from all our cultures toward becoming a more loving and just society.
2. Dr. King's concept of "beloved community" includes a commitment to love, nonviolent social action, and a truly caring society. For a more extensive overview of the philosophy and practice of beloved community, see www.thekingcenter.org or www.belovedcommunitiesnet.org.
3. Other immediate family members to note are Marcos's full family, including his wife, Robin, his oldest son, Canek, and his young daughters, Maya and Julianna. Canek's mother, Irene Peña, is also considered family despite her divorce from Marcos more than 15 years ago.

Introduction: Awakening to Activism

1. Among Latinos, those of us who identify as Chicanos are often Mexican-Americans who are committed to sustaining a connection to our indigenous culture, which, given our history, often involves a mix of values and practices from indigenous people from throughout the Americas. One of our cultural values is also to develop our social consciousness through understanding our historical origins and contemporary realities. *Occupied America: The Chicano Struggle Toward Liberation*, by Rodolfo Acuña (San Francisco: Canfield Press, 1972), and *Chicano Manifesto*, by Armando B. Rendon (New York: Collier Books, 1971), are excellent resources.
2. As a youngster I grew up within the culture and traditions of several Latino Methodist churches, affiliates of the United Methodist Church.
3. For an excellent resource on the Great Turning, see *The Great Turning: From Empire to Earth Community*, by David Korten (San Francisco:

Berrett-Koehler Publishers, Inc., 2006). In this book, Korten reviews more than 7,000 years of history to present how our evolving social and ecological crisis is a result of the "empire" form of society, which has dominated our planet for the last 5,000 years, and the choice we currently have to evolve what Korten calls "Earth Community," a society characterized by people working together to advance a culture and economic system that ensures the sustainability of our earth and well-being for all. Another resource is Joanna Macy, scholar of Buddhism and international voice of peace. For an introduction to Macy's explanation of the Great Turning, visit http://joannamacy.net/html/great.html.

Part I: The Family Perspective

1. James and Grace Lee Boggs, *Revolution and Evolution in the Twentieth Century* (New York: Monthly Review Press, 1974), pp. 19 and 21.
2. Stephen R. Covey, *The 7 Habits of Highly Effective Families* (New York: Golden Books, 1997), pp. 320 and 321.

Chapter 1: Making Family Your Cause

1. For example, Marcos's organizing activity led to a coalition of advocacy organizations that have influenced the passage of living wage ordinances that increased the wages of more than 5,000 families in Ventura County, California. The volunteer social work and prayer network maintained by our Mama Tita has uplifted the lives of many hundreds of people and families. The counseling centers Roberto cofounded have served thousands of families in the greater Oakland Bay Area. The combined cultural projects advanced by all the brothers have influenced thousands to appreciate the healing qualities of the Days of the Dead tradition and to see art as force for inspiring cultural and social change.
2. In regards to military service, conscientious objector (CO) is a status granted to people who have proven their opposition to serving in the armed forces and/or bearing arms on the grounds of moral or religious principles. During the Vietnam War, COs had two service options available to them: to serve in a noncombatant capacity within the armed forces or to serve in a job that made a meaningful contribution to the nation in terms of health, safety, or other public interests. A number of COs (such as ourselves) made a two-year commitment to organize and provide health care services for the underserved.
3. I joined the staff of *La Clinica de la Raza* (The People's Clinic), a community health center founded by student activists in 1971, which now operates with a $27 million budget and 19 facilities that serve the medically indigent of Alameda and Contra Costa counties. The mental health center initially called *El Centro de Salud Mental*, was cofounded by Joel

García, Ron Soto, Carmen Carrillo and myself, and was later named *Casa del Sol* (House of the Sun).
4. Many of these questions regarding vision, strategy, and the Great Turning emerged during a national convening of activist leaders I facilitated for the Positive Futures Network. This work is documented in a booklet, *Movement Building for Transformative Change*, by Frances F. Korten and Roberto Vargas (Bainbridge Island, WA: The Positive Futures Network, 2006). For more information, visit www.yesmagazine.org.

Chapter 2: Principles to Guide Family Activism

1. Phil McGraw, *Family First* (New York: Free Press, 2004), p. 7.
2. U.S. Department of Agriculture findings, reported by the Food Research and Action Center (FRAC), www.frac.org (accessed January 1, 2008).
3. Mahatma Gandhi (1869–1948) was a major political and spiritual leader of India and the Indian independence movement. He pioneered the philosophy and practice of *Satyagraha*, which he called "love-force." His work developed into a mass civil disobedience and nonviolence movement that gained India's independence and inspired movements for civil rights and freedom around the world.
4. Pablo Sanchez, the founding dean of the School of Social Work, San Jose State University, was a principle role model and mentor to many of the first generation of activist Chicanos to attend the university system in California.
5. Derived from interviews with Puanani Burgess, Native Hawaiian healer, Buddhist priest, and executive director of the Wai'anae Coast Community Alternative Development Corporation, Wai'anae, Hawaii.
6. Martin Luther King, Jr., "The Power of Non-violence," (1958), in *I Have a Dream: Writings and Speeches that Changed the World* (San Francisco: Harper Collins Publishers, 1992), p. 30–31.
7. Ibid., King, "Our Struggle" (1956), pp. 3–13.
8. *Porvida* is not to be confused with the concept of "pro-life" as used by antiabortion advocates. *Porvida* means to value all life, including Earth, wildlife, and all of humanity. Given this holistic perspective, one may be both opposed to abortion as a primary means of birth control and supportive of women's right to choose whether to complete a pregnancy.
9. Interview with Donna Graves regarding her extended family in Chicago. Donna's family has an extensive history of exercising family power within the family and community. Donna's mother is Mary Gonzales, principal leadership trainer for the Gamaliel Foundation (GF), whose mission is "to be a powerful network of grassroots, interfaith, interracial, multi-issue organizations working together to create a more just and more democratic society." The GF is widely recognized for its

social change leadership development program. For more information, go to www.gamaliel.org.

10. Marcos Vargas is founding executive director of CAUSE (Central Coast Alliance United for a Sustainable Economy), a research and policy advocacy center in Ventura, California, that works for economic and social justice.

11. Sharif Abdulla, *Creating a World that Works for All* (San Francisco: Berrett-Koehler Publishers, Inc., 1999).

12. "Heaven on Earth" is an idea popular within liberation theology, a school of thought originating among Latin American Catholics during the 1970s, which espouses that Jesus Christ's teachings demand that the church concentrate its efforts on liberating the people of the world from poverty and oppression. The role of the church should be to create heaven on Earth, to change the structures and ongoing processes of injury and oppression, and advance a society that is compassionate, courageous, and life-sustaining.

Chapter 3: The Familia Approach

1. *Razalogia* is a community learning process originated by Francisco M. Hernandez through his community work in California's Imperial Valley and the Oakland Bay areas during the 1970s. Roberto Vargas writes about the application of this approach in *Razalogia: Community Learning for a New Society* (Oakland: Razagente Associates, 1984).

2. *Conocimiento* (côh•nôh'•sï•myûntôh) is an intentional conversation between people to get to know each other in a respectful way. Doing *conocimiento* is essential to connecting, developing group power, and movement building.

Part II: Tools for Family Power

1. John Perkins, *Confessions of an Economic Hit Man* (New York: Plume, 2006), p. 261.

2. Phil McGraw, *Family First* (New York: Free Press, 2004), p. 9.

Chapter 5: Getting Your Act Together

1. Claudia Horwitz, *The Spiritual Activist* (New York: Penguin Compass, 2002).

2. Within ancient Mesoamerican cultures, including the Mixtec, Toltec, and Aztec, different views prevailed about Quetzalcoatl. To some he was a god and to others an enlightened ruler of the tenth century who advanced their civilization and originated a class of priests who taught reform. While virtually all the texts of this period were destroyed, the

oral tradition among various Mesoamerican indigenous people is that Quetzalcoatl taught by example that we have the responsibility to protect life, evolve a more respectful culture, and create social institutions that care for all people.

3. I want to acknowledge the activist commitment of Canek's mother, Irene Peña, for her conscious support of Canek's development by continually offering him opportunities to do his own self-discovery, and for maintaining her family and community activist commitments. Canek is currently working as a youth organizer while pursuing his career as an educator.

4. Anthony Robbins, *Get the Edge: A 7-Day Program to Transform Your Life* (San Diego: The Anthony Robbins Companies, 2000), tapes 1 and 2 of a seven-tape series.

Chapter 7: Co-powering to Battle EL NO

1. Marianne Williamson is a spiritual activist and author. Her famous quote, often incorrectly attributed to Nelson Mandela, is found in her book *A Return to Love: Reflections on the Principles of a Course in Miracles* (New York: HarperCollins, 1992), pp. 190–191.

2. Francisco M. Hernandez is a community educator and cultural activist recognized as the initiator of a powerful community education process called *Razalogia*, which means "learning of and for the people." This process is both similar to and different from the "popular education" approach taught by Pablo Friere, author of *Pedagogy of the Oppressed* (New York: Herder and Herder, 1972).

3. Williamson, *A Return to Love*.

Chapter 9: Learn, Communicate, and Teach

1. Albert Marabian, *Nonverbal Communication* (Chicago: Aldine-Atherton, 1972).

2. Dolores Huerta, co-founder of the United Farm Workers, organizer, and social activist, also speaks throughout the nation inspiring all people to engage in organizing. She does this work on behalf of the Dolores Huerta Foundation. Check her website for "Parenting Guidelines for Activists" at www.dolores-huerta.org.

3. Kapua Sproat is director of community education at the Center for Excellence in Indigenous Hawaiian Law and a professor of law at the University of Hawai'i at Mānoa.

4. Patricia Loya is executive director of Centro Legal de la Raza (Oakland, California), which is a legal aid center highly recognized for providing leadership in coalition building, community advocacy, and grassroots leadership development to create long-term positive change. Patricia

followed in the footsteps of her sister, Ana Maria Loya, who is executive director of Centro Legal de la Raza in San Francisco.

Chapter 10: Be the Facilitator

1. M. Doyle and D. Straus, *How to Make Meetings Work* (New York: Playboy Paperbacks, 1980).
2. Rebecca Victoria Rubi (1949–2007). Artist, poet, educator, and cultural activist, Rebecca was a relentless voice for justice within her local communities and the world.
3. Everett Altamirano Vargas (1910–1989). Oldest son, who as a child labored to support his family. He became a self-taught lifelong learner, longshoreman, model of healthy living (eating fruits and walking miles), artist, and father who made hard labor a joy to financially support his family.
4. In his article "The Porvida Approach: For Multicultural Respect and Organizational Success," Roberto Vargas provides a case study in which he uses many of the family council tools to advance the effectiveness and well-being of a major advocacy organization. The article can be found in *Re-Centering Culture and Knowledge in Conflict Resolution Practice*, ed. by Mary Trujillo, S. Y. Bowland, Linda James Myers, Phillip M. Richards, and Beth Roy (Syracuse, NY: Syracuse University Press, 2008). Similarly, the booklet *Movement Building for Transformational Change*, by Francis F. Korten and Roberto Vargas, provides another case example in which a number of these tools were used to design and facilitate council gatherings to build community among activist leaders from throughout the nation (Bainbridge Island, WA: The Positive Futures Network, 2006).

Chapter 11: Forming Unity Circles

1. Several years later, Blas commented on how the unity circle impacted his and others' lives. At least two family members shared that this was the first time they had ever been able to speak in a public forum. Using the talking stick helped them find their courage, which they have since applied to other aspects of their lives. Meanwhile, Blas often uses his talking stick to encourage student participation in the leadership workshops he conducts throughout California.
2. The applause made popular by the United Farm Workers (UFW) begins with everyone clapping in unison, beginning at a medium-slow pace and speeding up in tempo until it is a loud rapid beat that typically ends with several *"Vive"* shouts, such as *"Vive César Chávez"* or *"Vive la lucha"* ("Long live César Chávez" or "Long live the struggle").

3. María Ofelia Vargas (1941–1996). Educator, clinical social worker, tireless advocate for the rights and advancement of women, young people, and members of the Latino community, and cofounder of the Institute for the Study of Psychopolitical Trauma in Berkeley, California.

Part III: Moving from Family to Community Power

1. David C. Korten, *The Great Turning: From Empire to Earth Community* (San Francisco: Berrett-Koehler Publishers, Inc., 2009), p. 317.

Chapter 12: Creating Powerful Family and Community Gatherings

1. This specific ceremony event also involved recognition of the godparents for Tahnee, the daughter of Juan Camacho and Maria Aguilar.
2. *Votantes Unidos* (United Voters) was founded to empower citizens to become engaged voters. The organization provided citizen education and voter registration in Alameda County, California, between 1990 and 2002.
3. One of the meanings of *carnal* is "first cousin," yet among many Latinos it often means being "tight brothers" with a shared commitment to support each other and "have each other's back."
4. *Cultura*, while literally meaning culture, for many Latinos means "all that is positive and inspiring of our Latino/Mexican/indigenous culture," such as the love of *familia*, the nature of our relationships, our music, the feeling we have for community, etc.
5. While many men have participated in the Oakland Men's Council over the years, I would like to acknowledge several men who have consistently served as principle caretakers for the group, including Jerry Atkin, Kosta Bagakis, Terry Day, Andres García, Joel García, Alberto Lopez, Samuel Martinez, Antonio Ramirez, and Marcos Tapia.
6. For a general list of men's councils or support groups, visit www.mensweb.org or www.themenscenter.com. For information on developing councils similar in tradition to the Oakland Men's Council, contact the National Compadres Network at www.nationalcompadresnetwork.com. As more support groups are usually available for women, a Web search should identify a variety of local resources.
7. Document from the Oakland Men's Council, Roberto Vargas, February 1999.

Chapter 13: Expanding Family Action into Community Action

1. Jack Alen Vargas (1952–1995). Beloved brother and son, artist and gay rights advocate whose message was "Create beauty in all that we do."

2. The beautifully illustrated book *El Corazon de la Muerte: Altars and Offerings for Days of the Dead* provides tremendous insight into the Days of the Dead tradition and the Oakland Museum of California's ten-year history of organizing annual exhibits and celebrations for this occasion. Published by Heyday Books, Berkeley, California, 2005.
3. The Days of the Dead Committee became a spin-off of the Latino Advisory Committee to focus on year-round organizing to develop the annual Days of the Dead program. Their orientation is to develop programs that respond to the needs of the community while modeling the positive values of *familia* and community. While many should be recognized for the ongoing success of this program, Barbara Henry, the staff of the Education Department, and the Days of the Dead Committee chairperson, Joaquín Newman, have provided many years of outstanding leadership.
4. For more information, visit the website of the Center for Art and Public Life, www.center.cca.edu or www.museumca.org/press/press_100_families.html.
5. The Castro Valley Latino Education Association was recognized by the Alameda County Board of Education in 2005 for the leadership they provided in fostering student success and multicultural understanding in Alameda County. Special recognition is extended to Rochelle Elias, Clare Enseñat, Judi García, Carlos Navarro, and Teresa Tirado for their years of providing active leadership for this organization.
6. Rockwood Leadership Program provides state of the art training for leaders of nonprofit organizations throughout the nation. For more information, visit www.rockwoodleadership.org.
7. For more information, visit www.1000flowers.org.
8. Among the affiliations of the North Brier Family Network are staff or board positions at the As You Sow Foundation, Black Rock Arts Foundation, Center for Resource Solutions, Environmental Grantmakers Association, Forest Ethics, Funders Working Group for Sustainable Consumption and Production, Further Foundation, Greenpeace, Green Schools Project, International Accountability Project, International Rivers Network, New Place Fund, the Progressive Leadership Network, Rainforest Action Network, Restoring Eden, Rex Foundation, the Samdhana Institute, the Social Venture Network, and a dozen other nonprofits.

INDEX

ABOUT THE AUTHOR

R oberto Vargas, principal consultant for New World Associates, is an educator, planning consultant, and ceremony leader. Nationally recognized for his skills in meeting facilitation and leadership development, Roberto has more than twenty-five years of experience providing consultations on community problem-solving, multicultural team-building, and strategic planning throughout the United States, Canada, Mexico, and Sweden. His focus is assisting proactive organizations to become their best, and his clients have included colleges, corporations, public institutions, Native American reservations, and more than 150 agencies and organizations dedicated to community service. Founding director of several

Roberto with Andrea, Rebeca, and Ixchel, 2006.

counseling centers, his theory and tools for people empowerment, leadership development, and cultural activism are used by many.

Roberto cofounded *El Centro de Salud Mental* (Oakland, California, 1973), *La Familia* Counseling Services (Hayward, California, 1976), and a number of community advocacy organizations. He later taught community organizing and leadership development at the University of California at Berkeley and San Jose State University. As a ceremony leader, he draws from his indigenous traditions to help groups connect with spirit and become more "community." He also teaches families and groups how to create and guide their own ceremonies for occasions such as anniversaries, funerals, and weddings, and offers rituals for organizations, conferences, and cultural events to inspire greater vision, purpose, and unity.

In 2006, Roberto was recognized by KQED as one of the Bay Area Latino Heroes, which was affirmed by commendations by nearly a dozen San Francisco Bay Area legislators and political leaders. Soon afterward, he and his wife, Rebeca Mendoza, moved to Ventura, California, to provide support for his mother. Roberto continues providing consultation services while also serving the Rockwood Leadership Program as a leadership trainer. His masters degree in social work and doctorate in public health were received from the University of California, Berkeley.

ABOUT BERRETT-KOEHLER PUBLISHERS

Berrett-Koehler is an independent publisher dedicated to an ambitious mission: Creating a World That Works for All.

We believe that to truly create a better world, action is needed at all levels—individual, organizational, and societal. At the individual level, our publications help people align their lives with their values and with their aspirations for a better world. At the organizational level, our publications promote progressive leadership and management practices, socially responsible approaches to business, and humane and effective organizations. At the societal level, our publications advance social and economic justice, shared prosperity, sustainability, and new solutions to national and global issues.

A major theme of our publications is "Opening Up New Space." They challenge conventional thinking, introduce new ideas, and foster positive change. Their common quest is changing the underlying beliefs, mindsets, and structures that keep generating the same cycles of problems, no matter who our leaders are or what improvement programs we adopt.

We strive to practice what we preach—to operate our publishing company in line with the ideas in our books. At the core of our approach is stewardship, which we define as a deep sense of responsibility to administer the company for the benefit of all of our "stakeholder" groups: authors, customers, employees, investors, service providers, and the communities and environment around us.

We are grateful to the thousands of readers, authors, and other friends of the company who consider themselves to be part of the "BK Community." We hope that you, too, will join us in our mission.

A BK Currents Book

This book is part of our BK Currents series. BK Currents books advance social and economic justice by exploring the critical intersections between business and society. Offering a unique combination of thoughtful analysis and progressive alternatives, BK Currents books promote positive change at the national and global levels. To find out more, visit www.bkcurrents.com.

BE CONNECTED

Visit Our Website

Go to www.bkconnection.com to read exclusive previews and excerpts of new books, find detailed information on all Berrett-Koehler titles and authors, browse subject-area libraries of books, and get special discounts.

Subscribe to Our Free E-Newsletter

Be the first to hear about new publications, special discount offers, exclusive articles, news about bestsellers, and more! Get on the list for our free e-newsletter by going to www.bkconnection.com.

Get Quantity Discounts

Berrett-Koehler books are available at quantity discounts for orders of ten or more copies. Please call us toll-free at (800) 929-2929 or email us at bkp.orders@aidcvt.com.

Host a Reading Group

For tips on how to form and carry on a book reading group in your workplace or community, see our website at www.bkconnection.com.

Join the BK Community

Thousands of readers of our books have become part of the "BK Community" by participating in events featuring our authors, reviewing draft manuscripts of forthcoming books, spreading the word about their favorite books, and supporting our publishing program in other ways. If you would like to join the BK Community, please contact us at bkcommunity@bkpub.com.